Scott Foresman

Fresh Reads
for Fluency and Comprehension
Teacher's Manual

Glenview, Illinois

Boston, Massachusetts

Chandler, Arizona

Upper Saddle River, New Jersey

The Pearson Promise

As the largest educational publishing company in the world, Pearson is committed to providing you with curriculum that not only meets the Common Core State Standards, but also supports your implementation of these standards with your students.

Pearson has aligned the Common Core State Standards to every grade level of *Scott Foresman Reading Street*, our premier educational curriculum. This product provides an alignment of the Common Core State Standards to the Grade 4 assessment items in *Scott Foresman Reading Street Fresh Reads for Fluency and Comprehension*.

We value your partnership highly and look forward to continuing our mission to provide educational materials that fully satisfy your classroom needs.

PEARSON

ISBN 13: 978-0-328-72638-7
ISBN 10:   0-328-72638-9
6 7 8 9 10 V039 21 20 19 18 17 16 15 14

Contents

How to Administer and Score a Fluency Test

A fluency test measures a student's reading rate, or the number of words correctly read per minute (wcpm), on grade-level text the student has not seen before. You may want to use a copy of one of the "On-Level" leveled passages from the Fresh Read tests for this purpose. Make a photocopy for yourself of the passage you will give the student. (The pages in this Teacher's Manual have a scale of running numbers to make it easier for you to know how many words the student read during the fluency check, while the passages in the student edition do not have the numbers.) Make sure you have put the student's name and the test date at the top of your copy of the passage. Have a watch or clock with a second hand available for timing the reading.

Give the student a copy of the passage for the test. Note: The student should NOT have seen the passage beforehand; it is a "fresh" reading passage for the student. Do NOT allow the student to read the passage silently before oral reading.

Have the student read the text aloud. Do not have the student read the title as part of the fluency reading; it is not included in the running word count. (You may want to tape-record the student's reading for later evaluation.) Stop the student at exactly one minute and note precisely where the student stopped.

As the student reads orally, on your copy of the text mark any miscues or errors the student makes during the reading (see the chart on page viii). Count the total number of words the student read in one minute. Subtract any words the student read incorrectly. Record the words correct per minute score on the test.

The formula is: Total # of words read – # of errors = words correct per minute (wcpm).

You will likely want to keep the test in your folder for the student. You may also want to record students' progress on the Reading Fluency Progress Chart on page xi and/or the Individual Fluency Progress Chart on page xii.

How to Identify Reading Miscues/Errors

Using the passage on page ix, the chart below shows the kinds of miscues and errors to look for as a student reads aloud and the notations to use to mark them.

Reading Miscue	Notations
Omission The student omits words or word parts.	You can whip up ⓐ batter in a matter of minutes.
Substitution The student substitutes words or parts of words for the words in the text.	First, mix a tablespoon of baking powder ~~with~~ *and* a half cup of flour.
Insertion The student inserts words or parts of words that are not in the text.	The name depends on where you live ᴧ *too*.
Mispronunciation/Misreading The student pronounces or reads a word incorrectly.	This all-American food is *delicate* ~~delicious~~ and easy to make.
Hesitation The student hesitates over a word and the teacher provides the word.	But they go by other names as well, including <u>griddle</u> cakes and hot cakes.
Self-correction The student reads a word incorrectly but then corrects the error.	Slowly mix the dry ingⓈᶜredients with the wet ones.

Notes

- If the student hesitates over a word, wait several seconds before telling the student what the word is.

- If a student makes the same error more than once, count it as only one error.

- Self-correction is not counted as an actual error. However, writing "SC" over the word or words will help you identify words that give the student some difficulty.

Sample Fluency Test

Here is the passage marked as shown on the previous page. This is the "On-Level" passage from Grade 4, Unit 1, Week 1. As the student reads the passage aloud to you, mark miscues and errors. Have the student read for exactly one minute, and then mark the last word the student reads.

Name *Susan*   *9/4/2009*   (107)   **Because of Winn-Dixie**

Flapjacks

You may know them as flapjacks. But they go by other names as well, including	15
H griddle cakes and hot cakes. The name depends on where you live. *too* Still, most	29
Americans know a pancake when they see one.	37
This all-American food is *delicate* delicious and easy to make. You can whip up (a) batter	52
in a matter of minutes. All you need is milk, an egg, butter, flour, baking powder,	68
and oil.	70
First, mix a tablespoon of baking powder *and* ~~with~~ a half cup of flour. Next, beat	85
together the egg with a half cup of milk and a quarter cup of oil. Slowly mix the dry	104
(sc) ingredients with the wet ones.	109
Now your batter / is ready. Heat up a large frying pan and add two tablespoons	124
of butter. Pour spoonfuls of batter into the melted butter. Let the pancakes fry until	139
they are golden brown on the bottom. Flip them over and brown them on the other	155
side. Serve the pancakes hot with maple syrup, honey, or jam.	166

112 − 5 = 107

Total number of words read	**112**
Number of errors	**− 5**
Words correct per minute	**107**

Interpreting the Results

According to published norms for oral reading fluency, students at the end of Grade 4 should be reading fluently at 130 words correct per minute in text that is on grade level. This chart gives recommended progress toward that goal.

End of Unit/Grade		Reading Rate (wcpm)
Grade 4	Unit 1	95 to 105
Grade 4	Unit 2	100 to 110
Grade 4	Unit 3	105 to 115
Grade 4	Unit 4	110 to 120
Grade 4	Unit 5	115 to 125
Grade 4	Unit 6	120 to 130
End of Year Goal		130

If a student's reading rate is lower than the suggested progress toward the standard for his or her grade level, your notes on the student's miscues may help you determine why the rate is low. Does the student make errors that indicate his or her decoding skills are poor? If so, further instruction in phonics may be needed. Do the errors reflect a lack of comprehension or limited vocabulary? In that case, instruction in comprehension strategies and exposure to more vocabulary words may help. A lack of fluency may indicate a lack of exposure to models of fluent oral reading. It may also mean that the student isn't reading enough material at his or her reading level. Encourage the student to read more books or magazine articles at an accessible or comfortable level of reading for him or her.

Reading Fluency Progress Chart

Student's Name	Unit 1		Unit 2		Unit 3		Unit 4		Unit 5		Unit 6	
	Date	WCPM	Date	WCPM	Date	WCPM	Date	WCPM	Date	WCPM	Date	WCPM
1.												
2.												
3.												
4.												
5.												
6.												
7.												
8.												
9.												
10.												
11.												
12.												
13.												
14.												
15.												
16.												
17.												
18.												
19.												
20.												
21.												
22.												
23.												
24.												
25.												
26.												
27.												
28.												
29.												
30.												
31.												
32.												
33.												
34.												
35.												

Individual Fluency Progress Chart, Grade 4

Name _____

WCPM	1	2	3	4	5	6	7	8	9	10	11	12	13	14	15	16	17	18	19	20	21	22	23	24	25	26	27	28	29	30
165																														
160																														
155																														
150																														
145																														
140																														
135																														
130																														
125																														
120																														
115																														
110																														
105																														
100																														
95																														
90																														
85																														
80																														
75																														
70																														

Timed Reading/Week

Name _____

Read the selection. Then answer the questions that follow.

Beach Party

Deb shook the crumbs off her beach towel and started off across the sandy beach to	16
the lake. A strong wind was blowing, and the sun had disappeared behind black clouds.	31
Very exciting weather, Deb thought.	36
"Where do you think you're going?" asked her mother, who was busy filling a beach	51
bag. "That storm is coming in fast."	58
"Oh, Mom," said Deb. "Let's just stay till it starts to rain."	70
"No way," said her mother. "This is a dangerous place to be in a storm. Don't you	87
know that lightning is attracted to water?"	94
Reluctantly Deb turned back. Quickly they finished packing and then carried	105
everything to the car. Suddenly a flash of lightning lit up the sky, followed immediately	120
by a crash of thunder. Rain began to fall in big fat drops that came faster and faster.	138
"Just in time," said Deb.	143

Turn the page.

Answer the questions below.

1 What did Deb do right before her mother said, "Where do you think you're going?"

A carried their things to the car

B said, "Just in time"

C walked toward the lake *(circled)*

D shook the crumbs out of her beach towel

2 Which of these events happened last in this story?

F The clouds covered the sun.

G It began to rain. *(circled)*

H There was a crash of thunder.

J There was a flash of lightning.

3 In response to her mother's concern about the storm, Deb

A shook crumbs off the towels.

B helped pack up their things. *(circled)*

C left the bag out on the beach.

D checked on what time it was.

4 How did Deb's mother know that a storm was coming? Use sequence words in your answer.

First the wind began to blow, and then black clouds covered the sun.

Common Core State Standards

Questions 1–3: Literature 1. Refer to details and examples in a text when explaining what the text says explicitly and when drawing inferences from the text. Question 4: Literature 3. Describe in depth a character, setting, or event in a story or drama, drawing on specific details in a text (e.g., a character's thoughts, words, or actions).

Name _____

Read the selection. Then answer the questions that follow.

Flapjacks

You may know them as flapjacks. But they go by other names as well, including   15

griddle cakes and hot cakes. The name depends on where you live. Still, most Americans   30

know a pancake when they see one.   37

This all-American food is delicious and easy to make. You can whip up a batter in a   54

matter of minutes. All you need is milk, an egg, butter, flour, baking powder, and oil.   70

First, mix a tablespoon of baking powder with a half cup of flour. Next, beat together   86

the egg with a half cup of milk and a quarter cup of oil. Slowly mix the dry ingredients 105

with the wet ones.   109

Now your batter is ready. Heat up a large frying pan and add two tablespoons of   125

butter. Pour spoonfuls of batter into the melted butter. Let the pancakes fry until they are 141

golden brown on the bottom. Flip them over and brown them on the other side. Serve   157

the pancakes hot with maple syrup, honey, or jam.   166

This simple recipe has many variations. Some people use buttermilk instead of milk.   179

Others use yogurt mixed with milk. Some cooks mix whole wheat, cornmeal, or oats   193

into the flour. Of course, choices for pancake toppings are endless. Fruit, chocolate, and 207

whipped cream are just a few favorites.   214

How do you like your hot cakes?   221

Turn the page.

Answer the questions below.

1 What do you do after you mix the egg, milk, and oil?

   A pour batter into the frying pan

   (B) mix dry and wet ingredients

   C add butter to the frying pan

   D add buttermilk to the mix

2 For cornmeal pancakes, when should you add the cornmeal?

   F after you heat the frying pan

   G after you add the toppings

   H when you mix the wet ingredients

   (J) when you mix the dry ingredients

3 What happens right after you add butter to the frying pan?

   A You add the flour.

   B You serve the pancakes.

   (C) The butter melts.

   D Pancake toppings are endless.

4 For what reason must you flip over the flapjacks?

   F to get the batter mixed up

   G to let the frying pan get hot

   H to make all the butter melt

   (J) to get both sides browned

5 List the three main things you have to do to make pancakes. Use sequence words in your answer.

First, get the ingredients. Then, mix the ingredients, or make a batter. Finally, cook the pancakes.

Common Core State Standards

Questions 1–5: Informational Text 1. Refer to details and examples in a text when explaining what the text says explicitly and when drawing inferences from the text. **Informational Text 3.** Explain events, procedures, ideas, or concepts in a historical, scientific, or technical text, including what happened and why, based on specific information in the text.

Name _____

Read the selection. Then answer the questions that follow.

Missing Dog

Barry raced into the house, forgetting to close the back door. He was late for his	16
baseball game and didn't think about his mother's warning to keep that door closed so	31
that Happy couldn't push it open and escape.	39
Barry changed into his uniform and grabbed his mitt. He was about to leave the	54
house when he realized that he hadn't seen Happy. At the same instant, Barry noticed	69
that the door was not quite closed. He called for the dog, but Happy did not appear. He	87
checked the entire house, but the mutt had vanished. If anything happened to that dog,	102
Barry thought, he would not forgive himself, and nobody else in the family would either.	117
Barry spent the next hour searching the neighborhood for Happy. He asked all his	131
neighbors the same question: "Have you seen a little black-and-white mutt with big	144
paws and enormous ears that is really friendly?"	152
They all shook their heads sympathetically.	158
Barry had just started designing a LOST DOG poster when his mother's car pulled	172
into the driveway. He jogged over to her and was about to announce the bad news, when	189
he caught sight of Happy sitting in the backseat. His mother rolled down the window	204
and said, "Aren't you supposed to be at the baseball game?"	215

Turn the page.

Answer the questions below.

1 **What happened before the events described in this story took place?**

  A Barry played in a ball game.

  B Barry's mother let the dog out the back door.

  C Barry changed into his uniform and grabbed his mitt.

  (D) Barry's mother warned him to keep the back door closed.

2 **What happened right after Barry came into the house?**

  F He noticed that Happy was missing.

  (G) He changed into his uniform.

  H His mother took the dog with her.

  J He shouted for the dog.

3 **Why did Barry look for Happy in the house first?**

  (A) Happy was supposed to be in the house.

  B He knew that Happy had not left the house.

  C He did not have time to search the neighborhood.

  D Happy could open the back door.

4 **What caused Barry to think Happy had run away?**

Possible response: Even though his mother had warned him that Happy might escape, Barry had been careless and left the door open. When Barry could not find Happy, he thought of his mother's warning of what could happen.

5 **At the end of the story, what did Barry probably do next?**

Answers may vary. Possible responses: Barry probably hurried to get to the ball game; Barry probably asked his mother to drive him to his ball game.

Common Core State Standards

Questions 1–3: **Literature 1.** Refer to details and examples in a text when explaining what the text says explicitly and when drawing inferences from the text. Questions 4, 5: **Literature 3.** Describe in depth a character, setting, or event in a story or drama, drawing on specific details in a text (e.g., a character's thoughts, words, or actions).

Name _____

Read the selection. Then answer the questions that follow.

Rabbit Fools Coyote

Coyote was hiding behind a bush waiting for Rabbit to leave his hole. But Rabbit	15
was no fool. He knew just where Coyote was hiding and what he would be planning	31
to do.	33
One day when Rabbit left his hole, he carried a big bag and pretended that he had to	51
run slowly because the bag was so heavy. Soon Coyote overtook him.	63
"Before you eat me, please let me empty my bag," Rabbit said. "My children are all	79
sleeping inside."	81
Coyote laughed and grabbed the bag while Rabbit raced away. Coyote sat down,	94
looking forward to the delicious meal in the bag. He stuck his head and front paws	110
inside and yelled out, "YEOW!" The bag was full of thorny cactuses.	122

Turn the page.

Answer the questions below.

1 **Why do you think the author wrote this story?**

   A to convince the reader of an opinion

   (B) to entertain the reader with a surprise ending

   C to explain how to act in an emergency

   D to express a feeling and create a mood

2 **What did the author probably want you to think about Coyote?**

   F He was very clever.

   (G) He got what he deserved.

   H He should not have chased Rabbit.

   J He was too proud of himself.

3 **What did Rabbit do *before* he left his hole?**

   A He put his children into a big bag.

   B He ran from Coyote as fast as he could.

   (C) He thought of a plan to trick Coyote.

   D He asked Coyote if he could empty his bag.

4 **Do you think the author was trying to make you laugh? Explain by giving an example from the story.**

Answers may vary. Possible response: Yes, because Coyote screams when he puts his head and paws in the bag before I knew what was in it.

Common Core State Standards

Questions 1–4: Literature 1. Refer to details and examples in a text when explaining what the text says explicitly and when drawing inferences from the text.

Fresh Reads Unit 1 Week 2 SI

Read the selection. Then answer the questions that follow.

Letter from a New Home

September 5	2
Dear Nadja,	4
I've put away my things in my new room, and my posters are on the walls. Now this	22
is starting to feel like home.	28
I can see the mountains and lots of pine trees from my window. My mom says I can	46
take skiing lessons this winter, so I can't wait for the snow. There are a zillion places to	64
go ice skating and tobogganing. Who knows, maybe I'll even learn to snowboard!	77
Yesterday we hiked up a mountain path that led to a beautiful lookout. The land	92
stretched out for miles and miles across a canyon. Hawks were drifting in the sky, and	108
it was almost like a dream. My dad had brought a picnic, and we ate lunch there. It	126
was warm in the sun. By the time we got back to the car, I was tired and cold and my	147
muscles ached, but I slept well last night.	155
School starts on Monday, and I'm a little nervous about being the "new kid" here.	170
I just hope my teachers are nice and that I make some friends fast. If I could just	188
change one thing here, can you guess what it would be? You got it—you would still	205
live next door.	208
Your friend,	210
Rosa	211
P.S. Write back soon! You know how I love to get mail.	223

Turn the page.

Answer the questions below.

1 **Why do you think the author wrote this selection?**

   A to persuade the reader to move to the mountains

   B to entertain the reader with interesting facts

   (C) to describe what it's like to be in a new home

   D to explain why hiking is a great sport

2 **In the paragraph that begins "School starts on Monday," the author's purpose is mainly to**

   F give information.

   G ask a question.

   H describe a place.

   (J) express feelings.

3 **The author's purpose in the first part of the letter is to show that Rosa**

   A misses her friend.

   (B) is getting used to a new home.

   C is sorry that she moved away.

   D likes to ski.

4 **What did Rosa do *right after* she hiked up the mountain?**

   F went to sleep

   (G) ate a picnic lunch

   H wrote a letter

   J went to school

5 **Why do you think the author chose to write about moving to a new home?**

Answers may vary. Possible responses: The author wrote about moving to a new home because lots of people can relate to it. Many people move, and everyone has different feelings about moving.

Common Core State Standards

Questions 1–5: **Literature 1.** Refer to details and examples in a text when explaining what the text says explicitly and when drawing inferences from the text.

Name _____

Read the selection. Then answer the questions that follow.

Tornadoes Strike Three States

Friday, August 15	3

Last night, a string of tornadoes cut a thousand-mile path across Kansas, Oklahoma, | 17
and Texas. The National Weather Service reported that in some areas, winds reached | 30
180 miles an hour. | 34

Today, businesses are shut down across the three states. Trees and telephone poles | 47
are uprooted. Power lines are down. Many areas are expected to be without electricity or | 62
gas for several days. | 66

Early yesterday evening, the weather service put out storm warnings. A strong cold | 79
front was approaching a strong warm front, causing at least ten separate tornadoes as | 93
well as huge downpours. | 97

Many area residents are shaking their heads today. "I looked out the picture window | 111
at sunset and saw two twisters coming my way," recalled Mabel Brown. "I just grabbed | 126
my cats and raced for the cellar." | 133

As it turned out, the storm bypassed Mrs. Brown's home, but she had heard trees | 148
cracking and glass crashing. She sat under a table with her pets for what seemed like | 164
hours, she said. Actually it was just a few minutes. | 174

A day after the tornado had passed, Mrs. Brown said, "The neighborhood is a mess. | 189
Still, I'm grateful that everyone is safe, and their houses are all standing. On the whole, | 205
we were very, very lucky." | 210

Turn the page.

Answer the questions below.

1 **What is the author's main purpose in this selection?**

A to entertain the reader

(B) to inform the reader with the latest news

C to warn the reader about tornadoes

D to tell the reader how to survive a tornado

2 **Which of the following does the author use most to make the selection informative?**

(F) short paragraphs and varied information

G technical terms and scientific information

H weather facts and historical information

J complex paragraphs and geographic information

3 **What was the author's main purpose in writing the paragraph that begins "Early yesterday evening"?**

A to catch the reader's attention

(B) to explain the cause of the tornadoes

C to describe the area after the tornado

D to list problems the tornadoes caused

4 **Using sequence clue words, write two sentences about the events described in the selection and the order in which they happened.**

Possible response: First, there were a lot of tornadoes. Then, businesses were shut down, and people had to clean up.

5 **Give one reason why you think the author quoted Mabel Brown.**

Answers may vary. Possible responses: Mabel Brown may have been quoted to show what the tornado was like for a person who lived through one; to give a feeling of what it was like to be close to a tornado.

Common Core State Standards

Questions 1–3, 5: Informational Text 1. Refer to details and examples in a text when explaining what the text says explicitly and when drawing inferences from the text. **Question 4: Informational Text 5.** Describe the overall structure (e.g., chronology, comparison, cause/effect, problem/solution) of events, ideas, concepts, or information in a text or part of a text.

Name _____

Read the selection. Then answer the questions that follow.

Wish Comes True

Dear Diary,	2
When I went to bed last night, I made a wish. When I woke up this morning, I saw	21
that my wish had come true. A blanket of snow covered the ground.	34
Mom fixed me pancakes before I put on my warmest coat, gloves, and boots. I met	50
Lisa at Cobb Hill with my sled.	57
Sledding down Cobb Hill is more fun than any ride at the amusement park. I love	73
coasting down with the wind in my face and the sun on my back. It's a long trek back	92
up, but it's worth it!	97
After we'd been sledding awhile, we met up with Nan and Betty. They had a	112
toboggan, and we all went down together.	119

Turn the page.

Answer the questions below.

1 Which of these events happened last?

A meeting Lisa

(B) meeting Nan and Betty

C going to Cobb Hill

D sledding down Cobb Hill

2 Which of these events happened before the writer woke up?

F Her mom gave her pancakes.

(G) Her wish came true.

H She met her friends.

J She put on her warmest coat.

3 Why is Cobb Hill important to the story?

A It is where the narrator eats breakfast.

B It is where the amusement park is located.

(C) It is where the narrator goes sledding.

D It is where the deepest snow can be found.

4 What is the narrator in the story like? Explain your answer using information from the story.

Possible response: She is prepared because she wears warm clothes to go sledding in the snow. She is strong because she can make the long trek up Cobb Hill. She is nice because she has many friends with whom she can go sledding.

Common Core State Standards

Questions 1–3: Literature 1. Refer to details and examples in a text when explaining what the text says explicitly and when drawing inferences from the text. Question 4: Literature 3. Describe in depth a character, setting, or event in a story or drama, drawing on specific details in a text (e.g., a character's thoughts, words, or actions).

Name _____

Read the selection. Then answer the questions that follow.

Topeka Tess

No doubt you have heard tales of Pecos Bill and Paul Bunyan. The feats of Topeka	16
Tess are not so famous, not yet. Even so, there are people who brag about her out on the	35
Great Plains of these great United States.	42
Tess was born in farm country. In fact, her birthday fell right in the middle of the	59
biggest harvest of all times.	64
Tess came into this world like all babies, crying. However, her crying was different.	78
It was more like talking. "Please, oh please, Mama," she bawled. "Let me help Papa in	94
the fields!" When her ma said she couldn't because she was too little, Topeka Tess let	110
out a shout that could be heard from Kansas to Ohio.	121
When Tess turned two, she was harvesting her family's fields all by herself. At ten,	136
she mowed every field in Kansas.	142
By the age of fifteen, Tess was ready for her biggest challenge ever. One afternoon,	157
Tess's father got a call from a neighbor. Trouble was brewing. A giant swarm of locusts	173
was heading their way, gobbling up crops as they flew.	183
Tess set to work weaving a net. Then she waited for the swarm. When it arrived,	199
she trapped every last locust in her net. Better yet, she used the wing power of those	216
bugs to help her mow the fields. Is it any wonder Topeka Tess is the hero of America's	234
heartland?	235

Turn the page.

Answer the questions below.

1 **Which phrase *best* describes Topeka Tess?**

   A young for her age

   B loud and lazy

   C large but gentle

   (D) strong and helpful

2 **What did Tess have to do before she could catch the locusts?**

   (F) weave a net to trap them

   G harvest her family's fields

   H mow every field in Kansas

   J use the locusts to mow the fields

3 **Why is it important that this story happens in the Great Plains?**

   A Tess cries out as a newborn baby.

   B Tess takes on urban challenges.

   C Tess yells across the United States.

   (D) Tess is a hero for farm country.

4 **What problem does Tess face when she is fifteen?**

   (F) Locusts are eating up all her neighbors' crops.

   G Her mother will not let her help in the fields.

   H The net that she weaves does not work very well.

   J She needs to mow every farm field in Kansas.

5 **What three important events took place in the selection and when did they occur? Use sequence words in your answer.**

First, Topeka Tess mowed the family's fields. Then she mowed every field in Kansas. Lastly, she saved all the fields from the locusts.

Common Core State Standards

Questions 1–4: Literature 1. Refer to details and examples in a text when explaining what the text says explicitly and when drawing inferences from the text. Question 5: Literature 3. Describe in depth a character, setting, or event in a story or drama, drawing on specific details in a text (e.g., a character's thoughts, words, or actions).

Name _____

Read the selection. Then answer the questions that follow.

Subway Ride

Jen followed Nicky and her mother down a flight of stairs. Nicky's mother handed	14
Jen a token. Jen slipped the coin into a slot and pushed through the turnstile. Then they	31
all went down another flight of stairs and onto the subway platform.	43
Jen heard a rumbling that sounded like an earthquake. She was bracing for the walls	58
to start shaking, when a train roared into the station. It screeched to a stop in front of	76
them. There was a crowd waiting to get on the train. Jen, Nicky, and Nicky's mother got	93
on with them.	96
The seats filled up before Jen or Nicky could sit down. "Hang on to that bar," said	113
Nicky's mother, and Jen held on for dear life. The train began to speed up and then	130
entered a dark tunnel. Nicky said something to Jen, but she could not hear a word over	147
the rumbling of the train.	152
After a minute, the train came to another screeching halt. "Six more stops to the	167
aquarium," Nicky said.	170
By the time the train reached the aquarium stop, Jen was used to the noise and the	187
motion of the train. In fact, she had found her first ride on a Boston subway train very	205
exciting. She just hoped their visit at the aquarium would be as much fun.	219

Turn the page.

Fresh Reads   Unit 1 Week 3 A

Answer the questions below.

1 What did Jen do right after she slipped the token into the slot?

   A braced for the tunnel walls to shake

   B went down a flight of stairs

   C held on for dear life

   (D) pushed through the turnstile

2 Where does this story *mostly* happen?

   F at the aquarium stop

   (G) in the subway train

   H on the train platform

   J going down the steps

3 Which detail is *most* important to the plot of the story?

   A The subway makes seven stops.

   B The subway is located in Boston.

   C The train enters a dark tunnel.

   (D) The train rumbles and screeches.

4 Tell three actions from the story that show that Nicky and her mother know the subway better than Jen does.

Possible response: Nicky's mother gives Jen a token to use.

Nicky's mother tells Jen to hang on to the bar so she doesn't fall.

Nicky says how many more stops there are to the aquarium.

5 How does Jen change from the beginning to the end of the story?

Possible response: At the beginning, Jen is afraid of the sound

and motion of the subway train. At the end, she feels more

comfortable, and she thinks it's exciting and fun.

Common Core State Standards

Questions 1–3: Literature 1. Refer to details and examples in a text when explaining what the text says explicitly and when drawing inferences from the text. Questions 4, 5: Literature 3. Describe in depth a character, setting, or event in a story or drama, drawing on specific details in a text (e.g., a character's thoughts, words, or actions).

18

Fresh Reads   Unit 1 Week 3 A

Name _____

Read the selection. Then answer the questions that follow.

Picture Perfect

Kimberly sat on the carpet at the coffee table, trying to make a painting for the	16
student art show, but it wasn't going very well. She wanted to paint a picture of herself	33
doing a hand stand since the art teacher said the picture should be of something you	49
love to do.	52
In the first picture she painted, she looked as if she were standing on her nose. In the	70
second picture, she looked as if she had three legs. Now, in this last picture she looked	87
as if her neck were broken.	93
"Horrendous!" she said, ripping up the papers. "Focus, girl!" And she made another	106
attempt.	107

Turn the page.

Answer the questions below.

1 What was most likely the author's main purpose in this selection?

A to advertise a show of student artworks

B to persuade readers not to judge themselves

C to explain how to draw the human body

(D) to entertain readers with a story about a girl

2 Which statement *best* describes Kimberly?

(F) She does not like her paintings, but she keeps trying.

G She gives up painting because it is so difficult for her.

H She can very easily do hand stands and paint pictures.

J She is much better at painting than doing hand stands.

3 The author describes Kimberly's paintings in a way that

A teaches the reader an art lesson.

(B) makes the reader smile or laugh.

C creates suspense in readers' minds.

D makes readers feel tense or afraid.

4 How did the author help readers imagine what Kimberly's paintings looked like?

Possible response: The author gave details about the pictures and told how Kimberly looked in each one: standing on her nose, having three legs, and even having a broken neck.

Common Core State Standards

Question 1: Literature 1. Refer to details and examples in a text when explaining what the text says explicitly and when drawing inferences from the text.
Questions 2–4: Literature 3. Describe in depth a character, setting, or event in a story or drama, drawing on specific details in a text (e.g., a character's thoughts, words, or actions).

Name _____

Read the selection. Then answer the questions that follow.

The Earth Album

Tom woke up from a nap, remembering fall in Vermont. He had just had a dream	16
about maple trees in October, his favorite month. In his mind's eye, the trees were a	32
dozen shades of red, yellow, and orange.	39
Last October, Tom's family had spent a week at a lodge in Vermont. One day they	55
went for a walk that led them deep into the autumn woods. The trail ended at a river,	73
where they stopped to fish. Tom's dad cooked their catch for dinner. Of course, they	88
wouldn't be going back to Vermont for a long time.	98
Tom was glad he had put together a big photo album to help him remember the	114
important events in his life. He flipped through the pages until he reached a school	129
picture of his class from last year. Tom had a sad expression on his face, even though	146
his parents had not yet told him of their plans. Tom wondered whether any of his friends	163
were thinking about him right now. No, they were all probably doing ordinary things	177
like biking, playing baseball, or even studying.	184
Just then, Tom's mother stepped into his cabin and said, "I have great news. Captain	199
James says the spaceship is making excellent time. We will be landing on Planet Turnas	214
tomorrow morning."	216

Turn the page.

Answer the questions below.

1 **What was the author's main purpose in this story?**

   A to make the reader want to travel in space

   (**B**) to entertain the reader with an unusual situation

   C to express feelings about the main character

   D to inform the reader about space travel

2 **In this story, where are Tom and his family?**

   F staying at a lodge in Vermont

   G walking in the woods

   H landing on the planet Turnas

   (**J**) traveling on a spaceship

3 **The author includes the sentence, "Of course, they wouldn't be going back to Vermont for a long time." Why do you think the author does this?**

   (**A**) to give readers a clue that something has changed for Tom

   B to show that Tom is moving to a new school in a new state

   C to describe why Tom likes the woods best during autumn

   D to explain how visiting the lodge had left Tom unhappy

4 **Why do you think the author has Tom look through the photo album?**

   F to tell all the places that Tom has been

   G to reveal that Tom is good with a camera

   (**H**) to show that Tom is thinking of the past

   J to explain what Tom was dreaming about

5 **Why did the author wait to say where Tom was until the end?**

Answers may vary. Possible responses: The author may have wanted to keep the reader guessing about what was going on; to surprise the reader.

Common Core State Standards

Questions 1–5: Literature 1. Refer to details and examples in a text when explaining what the text says explicitly and when drawing inferences from the text.

Name _____

Read the selection. Then answer the questions that follow.

Brandon and Chuck

Brandon and Chuck had been best friends since kindergarten, and they saw a lot of | 15

each other, having playdates every other day after school. Brandon would go to Chuck's | 29

house or Chuck would come to Brandon's house; it didn't matter—either way, they liked | 44

each other's company. | 47

One day, recently, though, Brandon decided he wanted a break from Chuck, even | 60

though he still considered him his best friend. After school, while they were waiting | 74

for the school bus, Brandon remarked to Chuck, "I don't want to play with you today!" | 90

Chuck looked down at the pavement; he almost started to cry. | 101

"You don't want to be best friends anymore?" Chuck asked, looking up with a | 115

pained expression on his face. | 120

"No, that's not it," said Brandon. "I just need to be alone today; I need some 'space,' | 137

as my mom and dad call it. You're still my best friend." | 149

"If you phrase it that way," said Chuck, "I guess it's okay. I was pretty worried the | 166

way you said it at first." | 172

"Sorry, Chuck," said Brandon. "You're right; I could've said it better." | 183

"I get sick of you, too, sometimes, you know," Chuck said, playfully punching his | 197

friend's shoulder. | 199

"Thanks, buddy!" said Brandon, groaning. | 204

When they got home, the two friends went their separate ways. | 215

Turn the page.

Answer the questions below.

1 Why do you think the author probably wrote this selection?

   A to share information about how to apologize to someone

   B to persuade readers to have more than one best friend

   C to explain the importance of having some time to yourself

   (D) to entertain the reader with a story about two boys

2 What is most likely the author's main purpose in the first sentence?

   (F) to show that Brandon and Chuck have been best friends

   G to describe what Brandon and Chuck were like in kindergarten

   H to explain the meaning of the new word, *playdate*

   J to point out what time of day the two friends play together

3 The author writes, "Chuck looked down at the pavement." This is most likely to show readers that

   A Chuck dropped something.

   (B) Chuck has hurt feelings.

   C Chuck is careful by the road.

   D Chuck saw a bus coming.

4 Do you think Brandon treats Chuck fairly and nicely in this story? Explain your answer with details from the story.

Answers may vary. Possible response: Mostly. It's fair that Brandon wants to play alone one day, but it's not nice when he says, "I don't want to play with you today!" When he apologizes to Chuck, he is kind and fair.

5 "I get sick of you, too, sometimes, you know," Chuck said, playfully punching his friend's shoulder. Why do you think the author includes this sentence in the story?

Answers may vary. Possible response: The author wants to show that Chuck feels OK about not playing with Brandon, and it is funny for readers to learn that Chuck gets tired of Brandon too.

Common Core State Standards

Questions 1–3: Literature 1. Refer to details and examples in a text when explaining what the text says explicitly and when drawing inferences from the text. Questions 4, 5: Literature 3. Describe in depth a character, setting, or event in a story or drama, drawing on specific details in a text (e.g., a character's thoughts, words, or actions).

Name _____

Read the selection. Then answer the questions that follow.

Some Like It Hot, Some Like It Cold

When it comes to weather, the United States gets it all. Hail, rain, and snow fall | 16
in different parts of the United States. Even hurricanes and tornadoes hit parts of the | 31
country each year. Some spots, however, have bright skies on most days. | 43

Why do some parts of the country get freezing winters while others stay warm all | 58
year? The most important reason is their distances from the equator. The equator is the | 73
imaginary line that runs around the middle of the Earth. Places closer to the equator tend | 89
to be warmer. Alaska, in the far north, is freezing cold in the winter months. By contrast, | 106
Florida, in the South, stays warm all year long. The good people of Florida are very | 122
lucky indeed. | 124

Turn the page.

Answer the questions below.

1 **What is the main idea of the first paragraph?**

(A) The United States gets all kinds of weather.

B Some parts of the country get rain, hail, and snow.

C Some places in the country have bright skies.

D It is better to live in some states than in others.

2 **Which part of the United States tends to be the warmest?**

F the North

(G) the South

H the East

J the West

3 **What do you think is the author's main purpose in this selection?**

A to tell a funny story about the people of Florida

B to describe the worst weather in the United States

C to point out which locations are sunny all year

(D) to explain why some places are warmer or colder

4 **What is the main idea of the last paragraph?**

Places closer to the equator tend to be warmer than the ones farther away from it.

Common Core State Standards

Questions 1, 2, 4: **Informational Text 1.** Refer to details and examples in a text when explaining what the text says explicitly and when drawing inferences from the text. **Informational Text 3.** Explain events, procedures, ideas, or concepts in a historical, scientific, or technical text, including what happened and why, based on specific information in the text. **Question 3: Informational Text 2.** Determine the main idea of a text and explain how it is supported by key details; summarize the text.

Name _____

Read the selection. Then answer the questions that follow.

The Big Apple

It's been called the Big Apple and America's greatest city. By any name, New York | 15

City is big. Located on the Atlantic coast, New York City covers over three hundred | 30

square miles and is home to more than eight million people. More people live in New | 46

York City than in any other city in the United States. | 57

The Big Apple has some of the world's tallest buildings, biggest bridges, and longest | 71

tunnels. More than 150 New York City skyscrapers reach more than five hundred feet | 85

into the air. A football field is only three hundred feet long. At 4,260 feet, the center | 102

span of New York's Verrazano-Narrows Bridge is almost a mile long. That makes it the | 117

longest in North America and the second longest in the world. New York City also has | 133

four giant underwater tunnels for highways. | 139

To keep all these people happy, the Big Apple has one of the biggest city parks in | 156

the world. Central Park is 843 acres. It is an amazing place to spend time. It has its own | 175

zoo, its own castle, and its own lake. Visitors can walk, run, bike, ride horseback, | 190

roller-skate, ice-skate, and more. | 194

In case you were wondering, all those New Yorkers also produce a large amount of | 209

residential garbage, about eleven thousand tons a day. Remember, you read it here. | 222

Turn the page.

Answer the questions below.

1 **What is the main idea of the selection?**

   A New York City is as large as some states.

   B Some of the world's largest buildings are in New York City.

   C New York City is an interesting place to visit.

   (D) New York City is large in every way.

2 **Which of the following details supports the main idea of paragraph two?**

   F three hundred feet long

   (G) 4,260 feet

   H eight million people

   J 843 acres

3 **Which of these details would support the main idea of paragraph three?**

   A the number of bridges built

   (B) the number of visitors there

   C the amount of water consumed

   D the number of trees planted

4 **What is most likely the author's main purpose in this selection?**

   F to give directions for getting to New York City

   G to persuade people to move to New York City

   (H) to share interesting facts about New York City

   J to tell a story that happens in New York City

5 **What is the main idea of the third paragraph?**

New York's Central Park is huge and has many things to see and do.

Common Core State Standards

Question 1: Informational Text 2. Determine the main idea of a text and explain how it is supported by key details; summarize the text.
Questions 2–5: Informational Text 1. Refer to details and examples in a text when explaining what the text says explicitly and when drawing inferences from the text. **Informational Text 3.** Explain events, procedures, ideas, or concepts in a historical, scientific, or technical text, including what happened and why, based on specific information in the text.

Name _____

Read the selection. Then answer the questions that follow.

National Parks

Who is the biggest landowner in the United States? The answer is our government.	14
The landholdings of our government include huge parks, great forests, seashores,	25
lakeshores, and rivers. About one quarter of all state land is owned by the United States	41
government. That comes to 563 million acres.	48
The country's largest parks are in the largest state. Alaska has seven parks with	62
more than a million acres each. The biggest, Wrangell–Saint Elias, has more than eight	77
million acres. This park also has the greatest number of mountain peaks over sixteen	91
thousand feet high.	94
The world's oldest national park is Yellowstone. Some would say it is also the	108
most beautiful. In 1872, it was set aside for the people in the United States to enjoy.	125
Yellowstone is a huge park, with more than two million acres. It has about ten thousand	141
geysers and hot springs. The most famous geyser is known as Old Faithful. It spouts hot	157
water just about every ninety minutes.	163
More people visit the Grand Canyon in Arizona than any other national park. Each	177
year, nearly five million visitors come to look out over the canyon worn away by the	193
Colorado River. It's a sight nobody can forget. It is nature at its best. Grand Canyon	209
Park also has more than a million acres of land. What's more, it was one of the country's	227
first national parks, founded in 1919. What's not to love about our country's natural	241
treasures?	242

Turn the page.

Answer the questions below.

1 **What is the main idea of the selection?**

A Yellowstone, founded in 1872, is the oldest national park.

(B) The United States has set aside millions of acres of land for parks.

C The most unforgettable national park is the Grand Canyon.

D A good part of all state land is owned by the U.S. government.

2 **What is the main idea of paragraph two?**

F Alaska has seven parks with more than a million acres each.

G One park has the largest number of tall mountains.

H Wrangell–Saint Elias has more than eight million acres.

(J) The biggest state has the biggest national parks.

3 **What is probably the author's main purpose in this selection?**

(A) to share interesting information about national parks

B to persuade the reader to visit one of the national parks

C to tell an amazing story that happens in a national park

D to state an opinion about the very best national park

4 **What is the main idea of the first paragraph?**

The U.S. government owns more land than any single person in the country.

5 **What is the main idea of the last paragraph?**

More people visit the Grand Canyon than any other national park.

Common Core State Standards

Questions 1, 3: Informational Text 2. Determine the main idea of a text and explain how it is supported by key details; summarize the text.
Questions 2, 4, 5: Informational Text 1. Refer to details and examples in a text when explaining what the text says explicitly and when drawing inferences from the text. Informational Text 3. Explain events, procedures, ideas, or concepts in a historical, scientific, or technical text, including what happened and why, based on specific information in the text.

Name _____

Read the selection. Then answer the questions that follow.

Little Brown Bats

The most common bats of North America are little brown bats. Only three to four	15
inches long, these adorable bats are covered in fur except for their wings and feet. They	31
have short tails and medium-sized ears.	37
Little brown bats gather in groups called colonies. They sleep all day, and then at	52
sundown, they fly out of their caves and trees to hunt for supper. A little brown bat can	70
eat half its weight in insects during one night.	79
In winter, little brown bats hibernate. Their body temperatures lower. Their	90
breathing slows down. They sleep until warm weather and bugs return.	101
In late spring, the mother bats give birth. At three weeks old, the young bats are	117
starting to fly and feed themselves.	123

Turn the page.

Answer the questions below.

1 What makes it the right time for the bats' hibernation to end?

   A The young ones get old enough to gather in groups.

   B The nights become long enough for them to go hunting.

   Ⓒ The weather warms up enough for insects to appear.

   D The temperatures go low enough to make them hungry.

2 One effect of being in hibernation is that

   F the bats hunt before sundown.

   G the bats stop breathing.

   H the bats forget how to fly.

   Ⓙ the bats sleep all the time.

3 For what reason do little brown bats hunt at night?

   A They live in big colonies and have to eat in shifts.

   Ⓑ They are animals that sleep during the daytime.

   C They need to find half their body weight in insects.

   D They live in trees, so they can see in the dark.

4 Tell one statement of opinion drawn from the selection.

Possible response: The author calls little brown bats "adorable." You can tell this is how the author feels about these bats, but it is not a fact that could be proven.

Copyright © Pearson Education, Inc., or its affiliates. All Rights Reserved.

Common Core State Standards

Questions 1–4: **Informational Text 1.** Refer to details and examples in a text when explaining what the text says explicitly and when drawing inferences from the text. **Informational Text 3.** Explain events, procedures, ideas, or concepts in a historical, scientific, or technical text, including what happened and why, based on specific information in the text.

Read the selection. Then answer the questions that follow.

The Blobfish and the Leafy Seadragon

The blobfish is a strange fish that lives in the deep waters off of Australia. Because	16
it lives so far down, people almost never see it. In only the past few years have people	34
been exploring the deepest depths of the oceans.	42
Blobfish live where the water pressure is very high. Other fish can't swim there	56
because their bladders, which help them float, are filled with air and do not work well	72
under such pressure. The blobfish's body is like jelly. It weighs a little less than water.	88
This lets the fish float above the sea floor without swimming. The blobfish doesn't have	103
much muscle. It doesn't need it because it just waits for its food to float by in front of its	123
face. Its face has an odd look of sadness.	132
Another strange fish found in the cold waters off the coasts of Australia is the leafy	148
seadragon. The body of this fish looks like a piece of seaweed floating in the water. It is	166
green, orange, and yellow and is covered with leaf-like fins. Unlike many other animals,	180
it is the male that carries the eggs and hatches the young. These fish have no teeth or	198
stomachs. They eat only tiny shrimp.	204
The deepest oceans are full of mysterious creatures. Most likely, more amazing	216
creatures will be discovered!	220

Turn the page.

Answer the questions below.

1 **Why have people rarely seen the blobfish?**

(A) The blobfish lives deep, near the bottom of the sea.

B The blobfish has an ugly face that scares everyone away.

C The blobfish is hard to see because it looks so odd.

D The blobfish hides under the sand at the bottom of the sea.

2 **The blobfish can live all right without much muscle because**

F it looks sad.

G it must swim.

H it eats jelly.

(J) it just floats.

3 **According to the selection, other fish *cannot* live where the blobfish lives because**

A there is no food for the other fish to eat down there.

B the blobfish fights the other fish it meets.

(C) there is too much pressure for the other fish to swim.

D the other fish have to breathe air to live.

4 **What is a likely reason that the leafy seadragon eats only tiny shrimp?**

F Shrimp are found in the green seaweed where it lives.

(G) It lacks any teeth to catch or chew up larger animals.

H Shrimp are the only food it can get in the cold water.

J It has leaf-like fins to attract the animals that it hunts.

5 **Tell a statement of opinion from the selection. Explain how you know it is a statement of opinion.**

Answers may vary. Possible response: The author says the blobfish is a strange fish. This is an opinion because it tells what the author thinks about these animals. The word "strange" shows the author's feeling.

Common Core State Standards

Questions 1–5: **Informational Text 1.** Refer to details and examples in a text when explaining what the text says explicitly and when drawing inferences from the text. **Informational Text 3.** Explain events, procedures, ideas, or concepts in a historical, scientific, or technical text, including what happened and why, based on specific information in the text.

Name _____

Read the selection. Then answer the questions that follow.

Carnivorous Plants

An unsuspecting fly lands on a shiny, green leaf. In less than a second, the two parts | 17
of the leaf snap together. They get tighter. It's dinner time for this Venus's-flytrap. | 31

The Venus's-flytrap is perhaps the best known of all meat-eating plants. There are | 44
over six hundred species of these plants worldwide. The Venus's-flytrap and several | 56
others can be found in the southeastern part of the United States. | 68

These amazing plants mostly eat insects, though some have been known to capture | 81
larger animals, such as frogs. They live in swamps and other areas with poor soil. They | 97
get some food from the air and soil, as other plants do. The insects add nutrients to the | 115
plants' diet. | 117

Carnivorous plants come in different sizes, from tiny water plants to vines many | 130
yards long. Like other plants, many meat-eaters attract insects with bright colors or | 143
sweet smells. They also have different ways of trapping their food. Some plants have | 157
sticky parts so that when an insect lands on them it cannot get away. Other plants | 173
have slippery parts and so when an insect lands, it slides down into the plant and gets | 190
stuck there. Finally, some plants have suction traps. When the insect comes near, it is | 205
vacuumed in. | 207

It is good to know that these carnivores are no danger to large animals, like us! | 223

Turn the page.

Fresh Reads   Unit 2 Week 1 A

Answer the questions below.

1 According to the selection, what causes the leaf of a Venus's-flytrap to snap shut?

A a large animal coming near it

B rain or hail falling around it

C an insect or bug landing on it

D sweet smells floating by it

2 Which of these is a statement of opinion drawn from the selection?

F Meat-eating plants can be found in the United States.

G Venus's-flytraps are amazing plants.

H These plants live in swamps and areas with poor soil.

J Carnivorous plants come in different sizes.

3 What happens when an insect lands on a carnivorous plant that has suction traps?

A The plant sticks tight to the insect's feet.

B The insect slips down into the slick plant.

C The plant snaps shut around the insect.

D The insect is sucked up inside the plant.

4 What effects do the plants' bright colors and sweet smells have on some insects?

Insects are attracted to the meat-eating plants by those colors and scents. Then the insects turn into dinner when the plants trap and eat them up.

5 What happens when an insect lands on a carnivorous plant having sticky leaves?

The insect gets stuck there. It is trapped and cannot escape. Then the plant eats it.

Common Core State Standards

Questions 1–5: Informational Text 1. Refer to details and examples in a text when explaining what the text says explicitly and when drawing inferences from the text. **Informational Text 3.** Explain events, procedures, ideas, or concepts in a historical, scientific, or technical text, including what happened and why, based on specific information in the text.

Name _____

Read the selection. Then answer the questions that follow.

Crocs and Gators

If you have a hard time telling an alligator and a crocodile apart, you are not the | 17

only one. The animals do look alike. They both belong to the same family. | 31

There are ways you can tell the two animals apart. An alligator has a wide jaw. A | 48

crocodile has a pointed jaw. On the crocodile, one of its lower teeth sticks up over its | 65

lip when its mouth is closed. An alligator doesn't show its teeth. A crocodile is found in | 82

saltwater. The glands in its tongue can get rid of extra salt. An alligator has these glands | 99

too. However, they don't work very well, so the alligator lives in fresh water. | 113

A

B

Turn the page.

Fresh Reads   Unit 2 Week 2 SI

Answer the questions below.

1 You can conclude from this selection that an alligator and a crocodile

   A look nothing alike.

   (B) are related to each other.

   C need to be protected.

   D live in the same places.

2 From the information in this selection, readers can conclude that both alligators and crocodiles

   (F) can swim.

   G hear well.

   H see at night.

   J eat a lot.

3 What conclusion can you draw from the first sentence of the selection?

   A Nobody knows the difference between an alligator and a crocodile.

   (B) It is difficult for many people to tell an alligator and a crocodile apart.

   C There is only one difference between an alligator and a crocodile.

   D All the members of the alligator family have exactly the same features.

4 In the drawings, which animal is labeled B? Tell two clues from the selection that help you know this.

Crocodile. It has a pointed jaw and you can see its teeth.

Common Core State Standards

Questions 1–3: Informational Text 1. Refer to details and examples in a text when explaining what the text says explicitly and when drawing inferences from the text. **Question 4: Informational Text 7.** Interpret information presented visually, orally, or quantitatively (e.g., in charts, graphs, diagrams, time lines, animations, or interactive elements on Web pages) and explain how the information contributes to an understanding of the text in which it appears.

Name _____

Read the selection. Then answer the questions that follow.

The *Great Eastern*

In the early 1800s, steam ships first crossed the Atlantic Ocean, from England to | 14

America. Yet, to make this long journey, a ship could not depend on steam power alone. | 30

It had to use its sails too. The steam ships burned coal to make steam, and had to carry | 49

this coal on board. If the coal started to run out, the ship had to stop at a port so the | 70

captain could buy more coal. Sometimes, there was no coal to buy, or no place to stop, | 87

so the ship had to use its sails to continue its voyage. Also, with a lot of coal stored on | 107

the ship, there was hardly any room for cargo or passengers. | 118

In 1854, an engineer named Brunel started to build a bigger ship that could carry | 133

huge amounts of coal and thousands of passengers. Although Brunel's *Great Eastern* | 145

was the largest ship built at the time, the ship seemed to have bad luck. Brunel could | 162

never attract enough passengers to ride on it. Instead, the owners used the ship to lay | 178

telegraph cables and even as a floating advertisement board. Sadly, the *Great Eastern* | 191

was sold for scrap in 1888. Still, the great ship's design changed the way ships were | 207

built from then on, and people today still admire the grand old hulk. | 220

THE *GREAT EASTERN*	
When Built	1854–1859
Material	Iron
Design	Two bottoms so the ship could not sink
Weight	18,915 tons
Power	Two paddle wheels, one propeller, and 6,500 yards of sail
Time To Take Apart	200 men for 2 years

Turn the page.

Answer the questions below.

1 Readers can conclude from this selection that the *Great Eastern*

A made a trip from England to Australia.

B used much less coal than any other ship.

C was the third ship that Brunel designed.

(D) was never a success as a passenger ship.

2 The chart is *mostly* about the

(F) features of the ship.

G voyages of the ship.

H builders of the ship.

J accidents of the ship.

3 The owners of the *Great Eastern* most likely sold it for scrap because

A the ship was never able to float on top of the water.

(B) they could not make enough money from the ship.

C ships started to use steam instead of sails as power.

D they wanted to build new ships that were even larger.

4 Which conclusion can best be drawn from the selection?

F Brunel was better at designing railroads than ships.

G Brunel died before the *Great Eastern* was even launched.

H Brunel traveled on the first trip of the *Great Eastern*.

(J) Brunel built a huge ship that few people wanted to ride.

5 What did Brunel probably hope to achieve by building the *Great Eastern*? Explain your answer with details from the selection.

Possible response: Brunel wanted a big ship that didn't run out of coal and yet could carry a lot of passengers, so that people could travel long distances more easily. He probably thought that many people would use the ship.

Common Core State Standards

Questions 1, 3, 4, 5: Informational Text 1. Refer to details and examples in a text when explaining what the text says explicitly and when drawing inferences from the text. Question 2: Informational Text 7. Interpret information presented visually, orally, or quantitatively (e.g., in charts, graphs, diagrams, time lines, animations, or interactive elements on Web pages) and explain how the information contributes to an understanding of the text in which it appears.

Name _____

Read the selection. Then answer the questions that follow.

The History of Communication

For thousands of years, people have been communicating with each other—saying   12
hello, sending personal messages, and sharing important information. Yet the way that   24
people have exchanged ideas has evolved over time. Today, people use computers and   37
cell phones to talk to each other, but in the past people didn't have these inventions. So,   54
what did people in the past use to communicate?   63

First, before spoken language, people probably "talked" to each other through sign   75
language. Imagine a caveperson pointing to a lion and then waving the other way to a   91
friend to say, "Let's get out of here!" People have also sent messages by banging drums   107
and lighting fires for others to hear and see.   116

Writing was an invention that truly changed the world. The Egyptians, Chinese, Native   129
Americans, and Sumerians used symbols, or pictures, as writing. The Phoenicians were the   142
first to use an alphabet as we define it. Our alphabet and that of other European languages   159
grew out of this one. All writing was done by hand until the invention of the printing press.   177
The printing press made it possible to spread ideas faster and farther.   189

Over the years, many more other inventions came along, including the cell phone.   202
In the future, who knows how we will be communicating? One thing is fairly certain: 217
People will always find new ways to share ideas.   226

Some Firsts in Communication

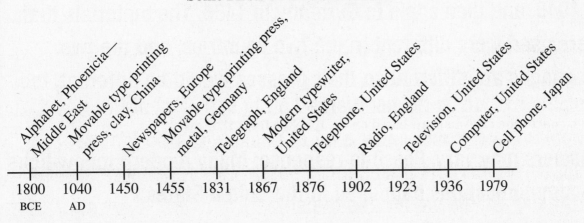

Turn the page.

Answer the questions below.

1 From information in the selection, you can conclude that our alphabet is most like the writing system of

(A) the Phoenicians.

B the Chinese.

C the Egyptians.

D the Sumerians.

2 Which conclusion can readers best draw from this selection?

F People communicate more on cell phones than on regular telephones.

(G) People are always coming up with new ways to communicate.

H People stopped writing by hand soon after computers were invented.

J People had started to write before they had ever started to talk.

3 The printing press most likely made it easier for

A people with a minor hearing loss to talk.

B more people to share individual messages.

C people to be the authors of longer books.

(D) more people to read the exact same words.

4 Which invention appears twice on the timeline? Explain why you think this is so, and support your answer with clues from the selection.

The printing press appears twice: it was invented first in China in 1040, and then again in Germany in 1455. The materials that were used were different in the two countries, and the two languages are different so their presses would be different, too.

5 What conclusion can you draw based on the timeline from 1867 on?

Answers may vary. Possible response: Many modern innovations in communications happened in the United States.

> **Common Core State Standards**

Questions 1–3: Informational Text 1. Refer to details and examples in a text when explaining what the text says explicitly and when drawing inferences from the text. Questions 4, 5: Informational Text 7. Interpret information presented visually, orally, or quantitatively (e.g., in charts, graphs, diagrams, time lines, animations, or interactive elements on Web pages) and explain how the information contributes to an understanding of the text in which it appears.

Name _____

Read the selection. Then answer the questions that follow.

Vet on Wheels

Jo Barns has six cats and two dogs. She used to dread their yearly visit to the vet.	18
Now, she just makes one phone call.	25
"I call Vet on Wheels," she says, "and they send out a vet who sees all my pets in	44
one hour."	46
Mike Roper has just one cat, but it's a fussy Siamese. Mike hated to take her to	63
the vet because she yowled the whole time. Now he too calls Vet on Wheels. "What a	80
relief," he says.	83
Vet on Wheels is the brainchild of Liz Wells, who has been a vet in Wayford, Maine,	100
for the last twenty years. People used to joke that she should make house calls. Then	116
one day she took the idea seriously. "I thought, yes, I should make house calls. It makes	133
people's lives easier, and it's good for their pets."	142

Turn the page.

Answer the questions below.

1 How did the Vet on Wheels customers probably feel about Liz Wells?

A angry

B fearful

(C) thankful

D worried

2 For what reason did Mike Roper feel relief when he used Vet on Wheels?

F He was able to have several pets seen in just one hour.

G He learned how to ignore his pet's unhappiness.

(H) He could have his pet treated more easily.

J He stopped getting phone calls from Jo Barns.

3 What is one reason Vet on Wheels is better for pets than going to a vet?

A They eat better at home than at a vet's.

B They don't have to see a vet so often.

C They see a vet who takes care of them.

(D) They aren't frightened by a strange place.

4 How was Jo Barns's life different after she started calling Vet on Wheels?

Now she could just make one call instead of spending a lot of time taking her pets to the vet.

Common Core State Standards

Questions 1–4: Informational Text 1. Refer to details and examples in a text when explaining what the text says explicitly and when drawing inferences from the text.

Name _____

Read the selection. Then answer the questions that follow.

Fun at Winston Park

Bobbie helped her dad spread the beach blanket on the grass and set up two beach	16
chairs. Bobbie's parents sat in the chairs. Bobbie sat on the blanket next to her little	32
brother, Sam.	34
Bobbie's mom passed around paper plates, chicken, potato salad, and cups of apple	47
juice. While Bobbie enjoyed her dinner, she noticed Winston Park fill up with blankets,	61
beach chairs, and half the town of Winston. Some ants crossed Bobbie's blanket. She	75
swept them off with her hand.	81
Bobbie's friend Mike passed by with his family. "You sure got a great spot," he said	97
to Bobbie.	99
"We come here every year," Bobbie told him. "We always come early to find a good	115
spot and have a big picnic."	121
"Well, I'll see you at camp tomorrow," Mike said.	130
When the sun started to set, an announcer asked for quiet. Then the band struck up	146
"The Star-Spangled Banner." Everybody stood and sang along as loudly as they could.	159
Some people could even hit the high notes. Then they settled back down and talked	174
quietly.	175
At last Bobbie heard the loud booms she'd been waiting for. The sky lit up with	191
giant sparkling flowers of red, white, and blue. Sam started to whimper and Bobbie	205
put her arm around him. Sam leaned against her and smiled as the sky exploded into a	222
million colors.	224

Turn the page.

Answer the questions below.

1 At what time of year did the story take place?

A winter

B spring

C summer

D fall

2 What word best describes how Bobbie felt about Sam?

F proud

G admiring

H sad

J protective

3 What caused the sky to be lit up at the end of the story?

A the glow from the park lights

B the bright moonlight

C the beams of their flashlights

D the colorful fireworks

4 How did Sam and Bobbie feel when they first heard the booms?

F Sam was afraid, and Bobbie was happy.

G Sam was sad, and Bobbie was angry.

H Sam was angry, and Bobbie was pleased.

J They were both happy.

5 How do you know that Bobbie's family had prepared for this event?

They came early with blankets, chairs, and food. Bobbie also said they came to Winston Park every year.

Common Core State Standards

Questions 1, 3: **Literature 1.** Refer to details and examples in a text when explaining what the text says explicitly and when drawing inferences from the text. **Questions 2, 4, 5: Literature 3.** Describe in depth a character, setting, or event in a story or drama, drawing on specific details in a text (e.g., a character's thoughts, words, or actions).

Name _____

Read the selection. Then answer the questions that follow.

The Big-Ring Circus

Nan's Journal	2
Saturday, May 8, 2010	6

Dad took Jesse and me to the Big-Ring Circus this afternoon. The gigantic tent was 21
packed with happy kids and parents, from the floor to the top of the tent. We were all 39
having a great time. 43

Soon the overhead lights dimmed, the band started playing, and the spotlights turned 56
on the circus parade. Riders on horses, elephants, and camels led the way. Dancers and 71
tumblers came next, followed by the hilarious clowns. 79

After that, two clowns stayed in the big ring. One clown kept falling down and 94
losing things. First he lost his hat, then his coat, and finally his shoes. The other clown 111
kept taking things out of his hat. He filled a giant bag with the things he pulled from 129
his hat. Then the first clown made a mess looking for his lost clothes in that huge bag. I 148
couldn't stop laughing the whole time, and neither could anybody else. 159

My favorite part was watching the acrobats. They climbed ladders almost to the top 173
of the tent. Then they started jumping from bar to bar. They swung upside down like 189
monkeys in a jungle. They did somersaults in the air. It looked like they were flying. 205
They also did tricks together. One acrobat would jump and another would catch her. I 220
kept thinking somebody would fall, but they never did. 229

Turn the page.

Answer the questions below.

1 Which words best describe the circus as Nan saw it?

   A small, loud, exciting, and funny

   (B) big, crowded, noisy, and exciting

   C silly, loud, strange, and sad

   D quiet, funny, crowded, and dangerous

2 For what reason did Nan go on laughing the whole time?

   F Dad kept on tickling her all through the circus.

   (G) Two clowns amused her with a series of silly stunts.

   H The animal parade started earlier than planned.

   J The acrobats continued doing funny monkey tricks.

3 How did Nan feel about the acrobats?

   A They should have been more careful.

   B They were very funny.

   (C) Their act was exciting.

   D They were afraid of falling.

4 What conclusion can you draw about the performances of the acrobats and the clowns? Explain your answer with clues from the selection.

Answers may vary. Possible response: The performers were very good at what they did. The clowns made everyone laugh, and the acrobats did fancy tricks that thrilled Nan.

5 Do you think Nan would tell her friends to go to the circus? Explain your answer.

Yes, because she seemed to think it was fun, interesting, and exciting.

4 Copyright © Pearson Education, Inc., or its affiliates. All Rights Reserved.

Common Core State Standards

Questions 1–5: **Literature 1.** Refer to details and examples in a text when explaining what the text says explicitly and when drawing inferences from the text. **Literature 3.** Describe in depth a character, setting, or event in a story or drama, drawing on specific details in a text (e.g., a character's thoughts, words, or actions).

Fresh Reads Unit 2 Week 3 A

Name

Read the selection. Then answer the questions that follow.

Tomatoes! Yum!

In summer, there's nothing as good as biting into a fresh, whole tomato. The juice | 15
drips down your chin, and the warm, sweet flavor excites your tongue. The tomato is | 30
the most delicious fruit on Earth! I always thought the tomato was a vegetable, but it is | 47
actually a fruit. | 50

The tomato is the most popular fruit in the United States. It even beats the banana, | 66
which is also an American favorite. | 72

Each person in the United States eats about 18 pounds of tomatoes every year. The | 87
tomato tastes awesome raw and is also great cooked, as in pasta sauce. | 100

The tomato is easy to grow. The United States grows tons of tomatoes every year. | 115

Tomatoes Grown in the United States in 2007	
California	12.6 million tons
Florida	557,924 tons
Others	238,864 tons

Most Florida tomatoes go fresh to market. Most California tomatoes are canned.

Turn the page.

Answer the questions below.

1 Which of these is a statement of fact drawn from the selection?

(A) The United States grows tons of tomatoes every year.

B The tomato is the most delicious fruit on Earth!

C The tomato tastes great raw or cooked.

D There's nothing as good as biting into a tomato.

2 The author writes, "The tomato is the most popular fruit in the United States." What is the best way for you to check that this is true?

F Ask your friends about their favorite fruit.

G Read a cookbook with some tomato recipes.

(H) Look up facts about tomatoes on the Internet.

J Find a chart about the history of the tomato.

3 Which of these is a statement of opinion?

A We each eat about 18 pounds of tomatoes a year.

(B) The tomato is easy to grow.

C Bananas are also a favorite American fruit.

D The tomato is actually a fruit.

4 What information provided in the chart is missing from the selection?

Possible response: The chart tells you where the most tomatoes are grown: in California and Florida. This information is not in the selection.

Common Core State Standards

Questions 1–3: **Informational Text 1.** Refer to details and examples in a text when explaining what the text says explicitly and when drawing inferences from the text. **Question 4: Informational Text 7.** Interpret information presented visually, orally, or quantitatively (e.g., in charts, graphs, diagrams, time lines, animations, or interactive elements on Web pages) and explain how the information contributes to an understanding of the text in which it appears.

Name _____

Read the selection. Then answer the questions that follow.

Best Job in the World

What is the best job in the world? Different people have different ideas. Some	14
workers want to make lots of money. Other people like a job that is easy. However,	30
many people look for a job they enjoy. Liking your work is the most important thing.	46
Different jobs make people happy in different ways. Many people work in the	59
"helping professions." These are jobs that help other people. Doctors and nurses are part	73
of this group. They work to keep people healthy. Nothing is better than helping other	88
people to feel better.	92
In a way, people in show business help others too. They get us to laugh. They help	109
us to forget our troubles. The ability to make others laugh or have fun is a great talent.	127
Maybe that's why dozens of new movies are made every year. Watching a movie is the	143
best way to forget what is bothering you.	151
Still other people enjoy making something beautiful or interesting. That is the work	164
of artists, singers, and writers. They make paintings, songs, and books. People should	177
spend more time looking at paintings. Nothing is nicer than listening to a good song.	192
Then again, reading a great book comes pretty close.	201
In short, you do not have to worry. There is a job out there for just about every taste.	220
That sure is lucky for all of us.	228

ACTIVITIES AND JOBS		
Helping People	**Making Things**	**Fixing Things**
Doctors	Artists	Plumbers
Firefighters	Writers	Road workers
Teachers	Jewelers	Mechanics
	Builders	Computer repairers

Turn the page.

Answer the questions below.

1 Which sentence from the first paragraph is a statement of opinion?

   A Some workers want to make lots of money.

   B Other people like a job that is easy.

   C However, many people look for a job they enjoy.

   (D) Liking your work is the most important thing.

2 Which sentence from paragraph 2 is a statement of opinion?

   F Many people work in the "helping professions."

   G Doctors and nurses are part of this group.

   H They work to keep people healthy.

   (J) Nothing is better than helping other people to feel better.

3 Which of these is a statement of fact?

   A The ability to make others laugh or have fun is a great talent.

   B Watching a movie is the best way to forget what is bothering you.

   (C) Artists, singers, and writers make paintings, songs, and books.

   D Nothing is nicer than listening to a good song.

4 Which job *best* fits in the blank space on the chart?

   F bread bakers

   (G) police officers

   H photographers

   J basketball players

5 What job interests you? Write a fact about that job.

Any response that includes a fact about a specific job is correct. Any response that contains an opinion is wrong.

Common Core State Standards

Questions 1–3, 5: **Informational Text 1.** Refer to details and examples in a text when explaining what the text says explicitly and when drawing inferences from the text. **Question 4: Informational Text 7.** Interpret information presented visually, orally, or quantitatively (e.g., in charts, graphs, diagrams, time lines, animations, or interactive elements on Web pages) and explain how the information contributes to an understanding of the text in which it appears.

Name _____

Read the selection. Then answer the questions that follow.

Fourth-Grade Sports Survey

Mr. Frank's fourth-grade math class took a survey of students' favorite sports. First	13
they made a list of fifteen sports. Then the students voted for their five favorite sports.	29
The winners were swimming, soccer, baseball, basketball, and football. These five	40
sports were used on the survey. Sailing is a great sport, but it did not make the list. Other	59
popular sports that did not make the cut were skating, kickball, and skiing.	72
All fourth graders at the Lake Shore School received a survey. There are 224 fourth	87
graders. The students had to pick only their favorite one of the five sports. It was a hard	105
choice. All five sports are lots of fun and exciting.	115
The survey found that baseball was the favorite sport of most students. In all, 63 of	131
the 224 students picked baseball. The number-two spot went to soccer, with 57 students.	145
Basketball was a close third, with 50 students. Swimming and football each received 27	159
votes.	160
The survey results seem strange to me. To my mind, swimming is much more fun	175
than basketball or football. Swimming is also the best way to get exercise. People can	190
swim year-round in an indoor pool. Basketball is the only other sport in the group that	206
can be played year-round in places with cold winters.	215
What is your favorite sport?	220

FAVORITE SPORT OF MR. FRANK'S 4TH-GRADE STUDENTS

Turn the page.

Answer the questions below.

1 Which sentence from the first paragraph is a statement of opinion?

   A First they made a list of fifteen sports.

   B Then the students voted for their five favorite sports.

   C These five sports were used on the survey.

   (D) Sailing is a great sport, but it did not make the list.

2 Which sentence from paragraph 2 is a statement of opinion?

   F All fourth graders at the Lake Shore School received a survey.

   G There are 224 fourth graders.

   H The students had to pick only their favorite one of the five sports.

   (J) All five sports are lots of fun and exciting.

3 Which sentence from the last two paragraphs is a statement of fact?

   A The survey results seem strange to me.

   B To my mind, swimming is much more fun than basketball or football.

   C Swimming is also the best way to get exercise.

   (D) People can swim year-round in an indoor pool.

4 What is your favorite sport? Write an opinion about it.

Answers will vary but should include an opinion rather than a fact.

5 Based on information in the selection, which bar on the chart is incorrect? Support your answer with details from the selection.

The bar for Football is wrong. It shows 50 students, but it should show only 27 students, as stated in the third paragraph.

Common Core State Standards

Questions 1–4: **Informational Text 1.** Refer to details and examples in a text when explaining what the text says explicitly and when drawing inferences from the text. **Question 5: Informational Text 7.** Interpret information presented visually, orally, or quantitatively (e.g., in charts, graphs, diagrams, time lines, animations, or interactive elements on Web pages) and explain how the information contributes to an understanding of the text in which it appears.

Name _____

Answer the questions below.

1 What is the main idea of the first paragraph?

A The Baseball Hall of Fame attracts crowds to view its large collection.

B The National Baseball Hall of Fame and Museum is in Cooperstown.

C There are more than 35,000 objects in the Hall of Fame museum.

D The Hall of Fame brings baseball history to life.

2 What is the main idea of paragraph 2?

F A group of baseball bigwigs got together.

G These important people carried out a three-year study.

H Many people shared their ideas about when baseball had started.

J Baseball began in Cooperstown in 1839.

3 What conclusion can you draw from the selection?

A Baseball is the favorite sport of most people in the U.S.

B All baseball players must give something to the museum.

C Many people come to see the baseball museum each year.

D Baseball players often sign baseball cards for their fans.

4 Why is the National Baseball Hall of Fame and Museum located in Cooperstown, New York?

It was found that the first baseball game was played in that city. So, that's where people wanted the museum to be located too.

Common Core State Standards

Questions 1–4: **Informational Text 2.** Determine the main idea of a text and explain how it is supported by key details; summarize the text.

Read the selection. Then answer the questions that follow.

Work Dogs

Does your dog sleep the day away? Is its only job to look cute? Does it only wake   18

up to eat dinner or play ball? Believe it or not, some dogs are not just pets. Some dogs   37

work for their living.   41

Many blind people count on dogs with special training. These guide dogs go   54

wherever their owners go. They help their owners move safely from place to place. They   69

learn to stop at busy streets. They help their owners stay out of danger.   83

Search dogs find people who get lost or trapped. Dogs have a much stronger sense   98

of smell than people. They use their noses to track down hikers lost in the woods. They   115

find people trapped in buildings after an earthquake. They help save lives.   127

Many dogs protect people and property. Some dogs are trained to watch farm   140

animals. For example, they may keep sheep from getting lost. Other dogs guard homes   154

and shops. Still others work for the police, helping to find people who have done crimes.   170

Dogs also have jobs in show business. You can see them on TV, in movies, in plays,   187

and in circuses. These dogs have to be smart and well trained. Circus dogs learn to do   204

amazing tricks. Dogs also show up in TV ads.   213

Whatever they do, though, whether as workers or pets, dogs are the greatest!   226

Turn the page.

Answer the questions below.

1 **What is the topic of this selection?**

A blind people

(B) working dogs

C guard dogs

D dog owners

2 **What is the main idea of paragraph 2?**

F Guide dogs get special training.

G Guide dogs learn to stop at busy streets.

H Guide dogs are good for blind people.

(J) Guide dogs help keep blind people safe.

3 **What is the main idea of paragraph 3?**

A Dogs have a stronger sense of smell than people do.

(B) Search dogs find people who get lost or trapped.

C Dogs can track down lost hikers by following their noses.

D Dogs can sometimes save lives.

4 **What conclusion can you draw from the information in this selection?**

(F) There are many different kinds of jobs for dogs.

G All dogs can learn how to be good work dogs.

H Guide dogs were the very first trained work dogs.

J Most dogs would much rather play than work.

5 **What is the main idea of the selection?**

Working dogs do many jobs to help people.

_____

_____

_____

_____

4 Copyright © Pearson Education, Inc., or its affiliates. All Rights Reserved.

Common Core State Standards

Questions 1–5: Informational Text 2. Determine the main idea of a text and explain how it is supported by key details; summarize the text.

Name _____

Read the selection. Then answer the questions that follow.

On Top of the News

Do you like learning new things? Do you enjoy meeting new people and finding out | 15

about their lives? Do you like to discover surprising facts? Do you think that writing is | 31

fun? If you answered yes to these questions, you might make a great newspaper reporter. | 46

A reporter writes stories for newspapers. Most reporters cover a "beat," such as | 59

sports, crime, or local news. Local news stories tell readers what is happening in their | 74

town. A flood, a train accident, or a new movie could be the subject of a story. Other | 92

stories cover news in other parts of the state, country, or world. | 104

How does a reporter get the facts for a news story? By talking to many people, on | 121

the phone or in person, and by doing research in the library or on the Internet. Reporting | 138

a story takes time and hard work. | 145

Reporters must find out whether their sources are reliable. They have to be careful | 159

and double-check their work. They have to make sure that their facts are correct. | 173

Finally, a reporter has to write the story. The opening, or lead, must be catchy to get | 190

the reader's attention. The body of the story must answer questions about the topic. A | 205

good news story ends with a kicker. This is a final statement that sums things up in an | 223

interesting way. | 225

Turn the page.

Answer the questions below.

1 **What is the topic of this selection?**

   A writing a news story

   (B) what newspaper reporters do

   C what to be when you grow up

   D doing research

2 **What is the main idea of paragraph 3?**

   F How does a reporter get the facts for a news story?

   G Reporters do research in the library and on the Internet to get facts.

   (H) Reporters talk to people and do research to get facts for a story.

   J Reporting a story takes time and hard work.

3 **You can conclude from the information in this selection that most reporters**

   A would rather talk to people than do research.

   (B) generally write about one particular subject.

   C have someone else check the facts for them.

   D only report news from the area where they live.

4 **What is the main idea of the selection?**

Reporters talk to people, do research, and write news stories.

5 **What is a detail that supports the main idea of the last paragraph?**

The opening, or lead, must be catchy to get the reader's attention.

Common Core State Standards

Questions 1–5: Informational Text 2. Determine the main idea of a text and explain how it is supported by key details; summarize the text.

Name _____

Read the selection. Then answer the questions that follow.

Lincoln's Family

Abraham Lincoln was the greatest President of the United States. He is known for   13
freeing all enslaved people in the nation. Lincoln was not only a great President; he was   28
a great family man as well. Lincoln and his wife Mary Todd had four sons. People often   45
said they were spoiled, because Lincoln always spent time with them, even during his   58
busy work day as President. I think he just really loved them. The oldest son, Robert,   74
went to college and became a businessman. Lincoln was very proud of him since   87
Lincoln himself had not attended college as a youth.   100

The family also loved dogs and other animals. They kept many pets at the White   115
House.   116

Lincoln's Family

Abraham Lincoln ___ (married 1842) ___ Mary Todd
1809–1865   1818–1882

Robert   Edward "Eddie"   William "Willie"   Thomas "Tad"
1843–1926   1846–1850   1850–1862   1853–1871

Turn the page.

Answer the questions below.

1 Which of these is a statement of fact drawn from the selection?

   A Abraham Lincoln was the greatest President of the United States.

   B I think he just really loved them.

   (C) The oldest son, Robert, became a businessman.

   D Lincoln was a great family man as well.

2 What year was Robert Lincoln born?

   F 1809

   G 1818

   H 1842

   (J) 1843

3 What was the name of Abraham Lincoln's youngest son?

   (A) Thomas

   B William

   C Edward

   D Robert

4 What information does the chart provide that the selection does *not*?

The chart has the names of all four of the Lincolns' sons and their birth and death years.

_____

_____

_____

_____

_____

_____

Common Core State Standards

Question 1: Informational Text 1. Refer to details and examples in a text when explaining what the text says explicitly and when drawing inferences from the text. Questions 2–4: Informational Text 7. Interpret information presented visually, orally, or quantitatively (e.g., in charts, graphs, diagrams, time lines, animations, or interactive elements on Web pages) and explain how the information contributes to an understanding of the text in which it appears.

Name _____

Read the selection. Then answer the questions that follow.

Inside the Earth

What do the Earth and a loaf of bread have in common? They both have a crust. | 17

Just as in a loaf of bread, the Earth's crust is the outer layer that is thinner than the rest. | 36

The Earth has four main layers that are different in size and material. The crust, made of | 52

granite and volcanic rock, is about three to five miles thick under the oceans and about | 68

25 miles thick under the continents. | 76

The Earth's crust is not one giant piece; it is made of many pieces called "plates." | 91

The plates float on top of the mantle. The mantle is a softer, movable layer below the | 107

crust. | 110

The deepest parts of the crust are 1,600 degrees Fahrenheit. That is hot! However, it | 123

is not as hot as the rest of the Earth. | 135

The mantle is thicker than the crust and is made of hot rock. It flows like hot | 152

pavement. Its temperature ranges from 1,600 to 4,000 degrees Fahrenheit. | 162

The core of the Earth is like a very hot ball of metals. It is 4,000 to 9,000 degrees | 181

Fahrenheit. The outer core is so hot that all its metals flow like syrup. | 195

The inner core is under three million times greater pressure than sea level. Because | 208

of this high pressure, the metals in the inner core are packed tightly together. It is truly | 222

rock solid! | 228

Turn the page.

Answer the questions below.

1 What *best* describes what the drawing shows?

   A The plates of the Earth's crust.

   (B) The four parts of the planet Earth.

   C The kind of rocks the Earth has.

   D The way the Earth's metals flow.

2 The drawing is probably included with the selection to

   (F) help you understand what the Earth looks like inside.

   G show you how a loaf of bread can be like the Earth.

   H help you learn about the countries on top of the Earth.

   J show you where your home is located on the Earth.

3 Based on the drawing, the mantle is

   A at the center of the Earth.

   B rounder than the outer core.

   (C) the largest part of the Earth.

   D just above the inner core.

4 You can tell from the drawing that the oceans are part of the Earth's

   F outer core.

   G mantle.

   H inner core.

   (J) crust.

5 Write a statement of fact from the selection. Explain how you would check whether the statement is true or false.

Answers may vary. Possible response: The selection states that the core of Earth is made of metals. I would check this fact in a science book or on a science Web site.

Common Core State Standards

Questions 1–4: Informational Text 7. Interpret information presented visually, orally, or quantitatively (e.g., in charts, graphs, diagrams, time lines, animations, or interactive elements on Web pages) and explain how the information contributes to an understanding of the text in which it appears.
Question 5: Informational Text 1. Refer to details and examples in a text when explaining what the text says explicitly and when drawing inferences from the text.

Name _____

Read the selection. Then answer the questions that follow.

The Water Cycle

Health experts advise you to drink eight glasses of water daily since it's good for	15
your health. That translates to about a glass of water every two hours. Imagine all the	31
millions of people on Earth doing this every day—that's a lot of water! Do you know	48
where all this water comes from? Your H_2O may have poured out of your kitchen faucet,	63
or it may have been spring or well water that was collected just recently; however, the	78
water you drink is older than that.	87
The water in your tumbler has actually been around since the beginning of the Earth.	101
The Earth has a limited amount of water. It just keeps going around and around! This is	116
called the water cycle.	123
The water cycle is made up of four parts. First, the water evaporates when the sun	138
heats up the water on the surface of the Earth, and this vapor, or steam, travels up into	155
the air. Second, the steam gets cold, changes back into liquid, and forms the clouds.	171
Third, when the clouds can't hold so much water anymore, the water falls toward Earth	185
as rain, sleet, hail, or snow. Finally, the water goes into the oceans, rivers, and lakes, and	200
soaks into the ground, and the cycle starts all over again.	215
The next time you drink some water, think about the fact that a dinosaur might have	230
drunk that same water millions of years ago!	239

1 — evaporation

2 — condensation

3 — precipitation

4 — collection

Turn the page.

Fresh Reads   Unit 3 Week 1 A

Answer the questions below.

1 The diagram shows the details described in what part of the selection?

    A Paragraph 1

    B Paragraph 2

    (C) Paragraph 3

    D Paragraph 4

2 The lower left arrow on the diagram shows how

    F waves on the ocean shoot like rays of the sun.

    (G) water vapor from the ocean travels up into the air.

    H the ocean rises at the same time the sun rises.

    J rain water falls from the sky into the ocean.

3 Which sentence from the selection includes a statement of opinion?

    A The Earth has a limited amount of water.

    B Second, the steam gets cold, changes back into liquid, and forms the clouds.

    C It just keeps going around and around!

    (D) Imagine all the millions of people on Earth doing this every day—that's a lot of water!

4 Why is the sun included in the diagram? Explain your answer with facts from the selection.

Possible response: The sun needs to be shown because it heats up the water on Earth, which then goes into the air as steam and makes the clouds.

5 What is one fact from the selection that is not shown in the diagram?

Possible response: The water from rivers, lakes, and the land evaporates and helps make the clouds too. It is not just the water from the ocean like the diagram has.

Common Core State Standards

Questions 1, 2, 4, 5: Informational Text 7. Interpret information presented visually, orally, or quantitatively (e.g., in charts, graphs, diagrams, time lines, animations, or interactive elements on Web pages) and explain how the information contributes to an understanding of the text in which it appears. **Question 3: Informational Text 1.** Refer to details and examples in a text when explaining what the text says explicitly and when drawing inferences from the text.

Name _____

Read the selection. Then answer the questions that follow.

Bryce Canyon National Park

Bryce Canyon is one of the most beautiful parks in the United States. It is in | 16
southern Utah, near Arizona. Everyone knows that the park has about a dozen horse- | 30
shoe-shaped canyons. They have many colorful rock formations. The rocks go from | 41
deep red to light pink to white in color. The rocks have odd-looking shapes. Some look | 57
like windows. Others look like arches and slots. Some crazy rocks even look like people. | 72
All these strange-looking rocks are called "hoodoos." | 79

Hiking at Bryce Canyon makes you feel as if you are in a magic castle. It is very | 97
exciting. The air is great to breathe too. It's cleaner than any air you've probably | 112
breathed before. On clear days, you can see for 200 miles, into three different states. | 127

BRYCE CANYON WEATHER SUMMER MONTHS			
SUNSHINE/CLOUDS	**June**	**July**	**August**
Number of Clear Days	17	16	16
Number of Partly Cloudy Days	6	10	10
Number of Cloudy Days	5	5	5

Turn the page.

Answer the questions below.

1 Which of these is a statement of opinion from the selection?

A On clear days, you can see for 200 miles, into three different states.

B They have many colorful rock formations.

(C) Bryce Canyon is one of the most beautiful parks in the United States.

D The rocks go from deep red to light pink to white in color.

2 Which of these is a statement of fact from the selection?

F It is very exciting.

(G) It is in southern Utah, near Arizona.

H The air is great to breathe too.

J Some crazy rocks even look like people.

3 Which sentence has a statement of opinion?

A The rocks are shaped like arches and slots.

(B) Hiking there makes you feel as if you are in a magic castle.

C The rock formations are called "hoodoos."

D The park has about a dozen horseshoe-shaped canyons.

4 Which summer month at Bryce Canyon would be *best* for seeing things far away? Explain your answer with information from the chart and the selection.

Possible response: The selection says you can see far on a clear day. So, you would want to be at the park in June because the chart says June has the most clear days (17) of any summer month.

Common Core State Standards

Questions 1–3: Informational Text 1. Refer to details and examples in a text when explaining what the text says explicitly and when drawing inferences from the text. **Question 4: Informational Text 7.** Interpret information presented visually, orally, or quantitatively (e.g., in charts, graphs, diagrams, time lines, animations, or interactive elements on Web pages) and explain how the information contributes to an understanding of the text in which it appears.

Name _____

Read the selection. Then answer the questions that follow.

Book Sale Starts Today

Have you read any good books lately? If you're looking for something to read, | 14
you'll want to visit the Adams School Library, where the exciting Fall Book Sale | 28
starts today and runs all week. Every year, students collect books from people in the | 43
neighborhood and sell them to raise money for a good cause. This gives you good prices | 59
on great books. | 62

When you walk in the door, someone will give you a large bag. Fill the bag with | 79
books, and pay only five dollars for the whole bag. These are the same books your | 95
friends have been reading, so you know they are good. | 105

There will be a special sale of new books on Tuesday. These books have been given | 121
to the school by bookstores. The prices on these are a bit higher, but still not as high as | 140
you would find in a store. You will not find a better deal anywhere. | 154

Money from this year's sale will help pay for a sidewalk from the school to the | 170
playground. This is important because, now, students have to walk through mud every | 183
time they go out to recess. | 189

If you or someone you know likes to read, come and check out this sale. The Adams | 206
School Library opens at 8:00 A.M. and closes at 4:00 P.M. Be sure to call if you have any | 225
questions, but don't miss it! | 230

BOOK SALE

ADAMS SCHOOL LIBRARY
Tuesday, March 31st – Friday, April 3rd
8:00 AM – 4:00 PM

Turn the page.

Answer the questions below.

1 **What sentence from the selection states both a fact and an opinion?**

A Have you read any good books lately?

(B) The exciting Fall Book Sale starts today and runs all week.

C Every year, students collect books from people in the neighborhood.

D These are the same books your friends have been reading.

2 **Which of these is a statement of fact?**

F You'll want to visit the Adams School Library.

G You know they are good.

H Come and check out this sale.

(J) The Adams School Library opens at 8:00 A.M.

3 **What information on the sign is *not* included in the selection?**

A the hours of the sale

B the place of the sale

C the reason for the sale

(D) the dates of the sale

4 **What clue words help you know that the following sentence states an opinion?**

"**This gives you good prices on great books.**"

F *this* and *prices*

(G) *good* and *great*

H *gives* and *good*

J *on* and *books*

5 **Explain how the following statement of fact could be proved true or false.**

"**Now, students have to walk through mud every time they go out to recess.**"

You could go to the school and look for mud.

4 Copyright © Pearson Education, Inc., or its affiliates. All Rights Reserved.

Common Core State Standards

Questions 1, 2, 4, 5: Informational Text 1. Refer to details and examples in a text when explaining what the text says explicitly and when drawing inferences from the text. **Question 3: Informational Text 7.** Interpret information presented visually, orally, or quantitatively (e.g., in charts, graphs, diagrams, time lines, animations, or interactive elements on Web pages) and explain how the information contributes to an understanding of the text in which it appears.

Name _____

Read the selection. Then answer the questions that follow.

Inside a Tree

Trees are wonderful the way they grow so high and spread so majestically; they are	15
like tall queens and kings that rule over the Earth. To me, trees look calm and peaceful,	32
staying in one place as they do all their lives. However, there is a lot that goes on beyond	51
the surface. The trunk of a tree is an interesting place. Let's examine the tree's trunk	67
from the outside in.	71
The outer bark, which can be rough or smooth, protects the tree from rain, heat,	87
cold, and insects, by creating a barrier between the inside of the tree and the outside	103
world. The outer bark constantly grows from within.	110
The inner bark is like a feeding tube for the tree. It is called the "phloem." The tree's	128
food passes up and down this part. The phloem does not live for very long. New phloem	145
grows, and the old phloem becomes part of the outer bark.	156
The sapwood is the tree's water pipe. Sapwood is new wood that moves water up	171
from the roots to the leaves. As sapwood dies, it turns into heartwood.	184
The heartwood is the center of the tree. It is dead wood, but still keeps its strength	201
and supports the tree. The heartwood is as strong as steel. A piece of heartwood the size	218
of a ruler, when standing up like a tree, can hold up twenty tons.	232

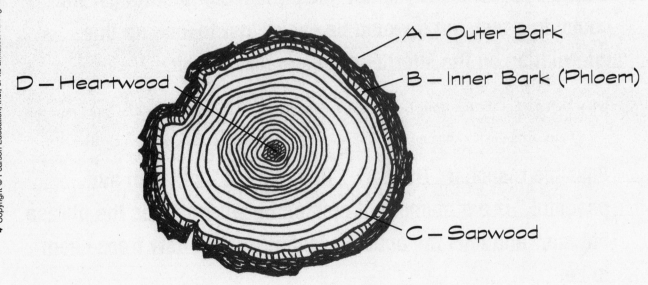

A – Outer Bark

D – Heartwood

B – Inner Bark (Phloem)

C – Sapwood

Turn the page.

Answer the questions below.

1 Which of these is a statement of opinion?

A The phloem does not live for very long.

(B) The trunk of a tree is an interesting place.

C As sapwood dies, it turns into heartwood.

D The outer bark can be rough or smooth.

2 What clue word helps you know that the following is a statement of opinion?

"Trees are wonderful the way they grow so high…"

(F) wonderful

G way

H grow

J high

3 Based on the diagram, which statement about sapwood is correct?

A The sapwood is right under the outer bark.

B The sapwood is in the very center of the tree.

C The sapwood is made up of four parts.

(D) The sapwood is thicker than the outer bark.

4 How would you prove whether this statement of fact is true or false?

"A piece of heartwood the size of a ruler, when standing up like a tree, can hold up twenty tons."

Possible response: If you had the equipment and things, you could do a test, but it would be easier just to look up this information on the Internet or in a science book.

5 Tell which part of the following sentence is a statement of opinion. Explain how you know this.

"To me, trees look calm and peaceful, staying in one place as they do all their lives."

Possible response: The part, "To me, trees look calm and peaceful," is a statement of opinion because it uses the phrase "to me," and tells the author's feelings about how trees seem to be.

Common Core State Standards

Questions 1, 2, 4, 5: Informational Text 1. Refer to details and examples in a text when explaining what the text says explicitly and when drawing inferences from the text. Question 3: Informational Text 7. Interpret information presented visually, orally, or quantitatively (e.g., in charts, graphs, diagrams, time lines, animations, or interactive elements on Web pages) and explain how the information contributes to an understanding of the text in which it appears.

Name _____

Read the selection. Then answer the questions that follow.

Owls

Owls live in most countries of the world. They are meat-eaters and hunt insects or | 15

small animals. The feathers on an owl's wings are soft and loose. This helps the owl fly | 32

without sound and makes it a good hunter. A few owls hunt during the day, but most are | 50

creatures of the night. They have sharp hearing, so they can find their prey in the dark. | 67

The littlest owl is about the size of your hand, from wrist to fingertip. It is the elf | 85

owl. It lives in deserts of the southwestern United States. Most owls are bigger, though. | 100

One of the largest is the great gray owl. Standing beside you, it would reach your waist | 117

or even higher. | 120

Turn the page.

Answer the questions below.

1 What clue word tells you that the following sentence is a generalization?

"Owls live in most countries of the world."

A   live

(B)   most

C   countries

D   world

2 You can conclude from the selection that when an owl hunts,

(F)   its prey does not hear the owl coming.

G   the owl does not fly home with its prey.

H   it hunts in large groups with other owls.

J   the owl's wings become harder and tighter.

3 What generalization can readers make from this selection?

A   All owls hunt at night.

B   Most owls live in deserts.

(C)   Owls are different sizes.

D   Few owls are hunters.

4 What generalization can you make about elf owls?

Answers may vary. Possible responses: Elf owls are the smallest owls in the world. Elf owls live in the desert.

Common Core State Standards

Questions 1–4: Informational Text 1. Refer to details and examples in a text when explaining what the text says explicitly and when drawing inferences from the text.

Name _____

Read the selection. Then answer the questions that follow.

Potters, Diggers, Hornets, and Yellow Jackets

What's that round, gray clump stuck to the wall outside your window? It looks like	15
a round ball of dried mud, but it's buzzing! Wait—something is crawling out of it. It's a	33
wasp, and that clump is its nest.	40
There are about twenty-five thousand different types of wasps. Most experts divide	52
them into two groups: social and solitary wasps. Social wasps build nests out of chewed	67
wood, like the one described above. Inside the nest, there are tiny pockets for wasps and	83
their eggs. Hundreds of insects may live in one nest, and the nest may be several inches	100
across. Hornets, yellow jackets, and paper wasps are all social wasps.	111
Solitary wasps like to do things their own way. They don't share their nests with	126
hundreds of other wasps. They build smaller nests for their own families. Some, like the	141
diggers, make homes in the ground or in rotting wood. Potter wasps use mud to build	157
tiny "pots" on bushes or trees.	163
All wasps are alike in certain ways. Adults have a body that is divided into two	179
parts, with a narrow part in the middle. They have six legs and mouths that can chew or	197
drink.	198
Most have stingers that are used to protect themselves and their eggs. A wasp sting	213
hurts because it contains a small amount of poison. Most wasps also have four wings,	228
and many are beautiful, with stripes and bright colors.	237

Turn the page.

Answer the questions below.

1 What clue word tells you that the following statement is a generalization?

"All wasps are alike in certain ways."

(A) all

B are

C alike

D ways

2 Which statement from the selection is a generalization?

F "It's a wasp, and that clump is its nest."

G "There are about twenty-five thousand different types of wasps."

H "Inside the nest, there are tiny pockets for wasps and their eggs."

(J) "Most have stingers that are used to protect themselves and their eggs."

3 Potter wasps get their name from the

A way that they eat mud.

(B) kind of nests they make.

C size of their families.

D ground that they live in.

4 What generalization can readers make about solitary wasps?

(F) Solitary wasps live in small groups.

G Solitary wasps build nests from mud.

H Solitary wasps sting each other.

J Solitary wasps eat wood.

5 Write three generalizations about the bodies of wasps.

Possible responses: They have stingers with poison, two part bodies, six legs, and four wings.

Common Core State Standards

Questions 1–5: Informational Text 1. Refer to details and examples in a text when explaining what the text says explicitly and when drawing inferences from the text.

Name _____

Read the selection. Then answer the questions that follow.

What Is a Glacier?

In the world's coldest places, snow almost never melts. Year after year, it piles up.	15
Pressing down on itself, the snow turns into ice. Then the heavy ice begins to slide	31
downhill. This moving ice, this "river of ice," is called a *glacier*.	43
You cannot see a glacier move. It is much too slow. The fastest ones move less than	60
the length of a football field in a day. Most move much more slowly.	74
You might think you would find glaciers only at the North and South Poles, but that	90
is not true. Every continent except Australia has glaciers.	99
Some form high in the mountains, where it is cold all year long. The ice in these	116
glaciers slides down the mountain very slowly. When it reaches warmer air, it melts.	130
While ice is melting near the bottom, more snow falls at the top. More snow turns into	147
ice, while always sliding down. In this way, the glacier flows like a river.	161
Some glaciers are great sheets of ice that cover the land. The ice sheet in Antarctica	177
is the world's largest. It covers millions of square miles. While it moves very slowly,	192
smaller glaciers flow inside it. The smaller ones move faster, flowing to the ocean.	206
There, they drop great blocks of ice into the sea. These blocks of ice are icebergs, like	223
the one that sank the *Titanic*.	229

Turn the page.

Answer the questions below.

1 Which of these sentences is a generalization?
(A) Some glaciers are very large.
B Antarctica has the largest ice sheet.
C One ice sheet covers millions of square miles.
D The Titanic hit an iceberg.

2 Why does the ice begin to move downhill?
F It starts to turn into snow.
(G) It becomes very heavy.
H It gets hit by an iceberg.
J It must drop into the sea.

3 Which of these is a valid generalization?
A Snow never melts in the mountains.
B All glaciers are at the north pole.
(C) Glaciers form in very cold places.
D Glaciers never move.

4 What valid generalization can you make about icebergs?

Possible answer: Icebergs have caused many ships to sink.

_____

_____

_____

5 What is the first generalization in this selection?

The first sentence: In the world's coldest places, snow almost never melts.

_____

Common Core State Standards

Questions 1–5: Informational Text 1. Refer to details and examples in a text when explaining what the text says explicitly and when drawing inferences from the text.

Name _____

Read the selection. Then answer the questions that follow.

Rosa Lopez Reads Again!

Rosa's teacher often told her class, "Reading builds a good mind." Books filled her	14
room so that students would have plenty to read. She kept charts on her desk like the one	32
you see below. There was a chart for each student. When students wanted to borrow a	48
book, they would keep a record on their chart.	57
Rosa Lopez came up to her teacher's desk with a book in her hand. She made a note	75
on her chart and gave it to her teacher. Her teacher read it and asked, "Do you know how	94
to ride horses, Rosa?"	98
"Yes," Rosa said. "My aunt lives on a ranch, and she showed me how to ride the	115
horses there."	117

ROSA LOPEZ				
Date Borrowed	**Date Returned**	**Title**	**Author**	**Comments**
August 30	September 9	A Horse Named Storm	Lee Carson	Great story!
September 9	September 28	Maggie's Wild Horse	G. West	Sad ending
October 6		Horse Families	Anna Rubio	

Turn the page.

Answer the questions below.

1 Why did Rosa's teacher ask her if she knew how to ride horses?

   A Her teacher gave horseback riding lessons.

   B Her teacher wanted Rosa to learn to ride.

   C Rosa often talked about riding horses.

   (D) All the books Rosa borrowed were about horses.

2 For what reason had Rosa's teacher filled the classroom with books?

   F She did not have a place at home for all her books.

   (G) She wanted her students to have plenty of books to read.

   H She thought Rosa was not reading enough books.

   J She made sure that she kept a record of all her books.

3 What effect does Rosa's aunt have on Rosa?

   A She gets Rosa excited about school.

   B She teaches Rosa how to read.

   (C) She gets Rosa interested in horses.

   D She helps Rosa find more books.

4 What does the chart tell you about Rosa?

It tells how many books Rosa read and that Rosa liked reading about horses.

Common Core State Standards

Questions 1–3: Literature 1. Refer to details and examples in a text when explaining what the text says explicitly and when drawing inferences from the text. **Question 4: Literature 3.** Describe in depth a character, setting, or event in a story or drama, drawing on specific details in a text (e.g., a character's thoughts, words, or actions).

Fresh Reads Unit 3 Week 4 SI

Name _____

Read the selection. Then answer the questions that follow.

The Shy Octopus

Crawling fast across the ocean floor, an octopus looks for a hiding place. It finds | 15

a crab in the sand and eats it. Then the octopus settles into a small hole among some | 33

rocks. Its skin changes color to match the rocks, helping it hide. Feeling safe, the | 48

octopus looks around for food. | 53

A minute later, an eel frightens the shy octopus. The octopus shoots a cloud of dark | 69

liquid into the water. Under cover of its "ink cloud," the octopus hurries away. | 83

The octopus has two large eyes. It can see very well. This helps it hunt for food and | 101

look out for its enemies. It has a soft body with a head, a trunk, and a "skirt." Eight arms | 121

are connected to the skirt. There are two rows of suckers on each arm. In the center of | 139

the skirt is a mouth like a beak. | 147

The octopus can move in two different ways. It can use its long arms to pull itself | 164

along, or it can use its siphon. The siphon is a sort of tube. The octopus pushes water out | 183

of the tube, and as the water shoots out one way, the octopus shoots off in the other. | 201

The octopus lives in all of the oceans except the Arctic. Some octopuses are small, | 216

only a few inches in length. Others grow to be as long as a car. | 231

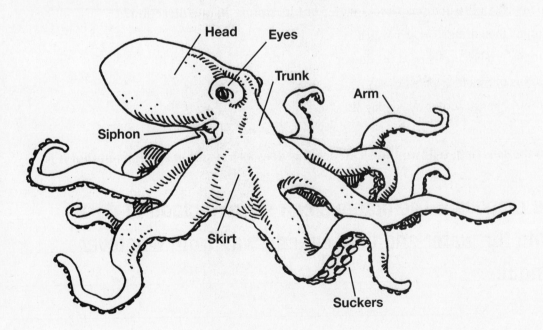

Turn the page.

Answer the questions below.

1 For what reason does an octopus shoot out an "ink cloud"?

   A It is lonely and needs company.

   B It is hungry and needs to eat.

   C It is tired and needs darkness.

   (D) It is afraid and needs to hide.

2 Where are the octopus's eyes?

   F in the center of the skirt

   G near the bottom of the trunk

   (H) above the siphon

   J at the end of an arm

3 What happens because the octopus has changed its color?

   (A) Its body then matches the rocks.

   B It can then find food for itself.

   C Its eyes then look out for enemies.

   D It then swims into a small hole.

4 What happens when the octopus shoots water out its siphon in one direction?

   F The octopus then drinks cleaner water.

   G The octopus washes up its food for dinner.

   (H) The octopus moves the opposite way.

   J The octopus changes color by rinsing its skin.

5 Based upon the selection, tell two things an octopus does as a result of finding out that it is in danger.

Possible response: The octopus can shoot a cloud of dark liquid into the water and then speed away from whatever is scaring it.

Common Core State Standards

Questions 1, 3–5: Informational Text 1. Refer to details and examples in a text when explaining what the text says explicitly and when drawing inferences from the text. **Question 2: Informational Text 7.** Interpret information presented visually, orally, or quantitatively (e.g., in charts, graphs, diagrams, time lines, animations, or interactive elements on Web pages) and explain how the information contributes to an understanding of the text in which it appears.

Name _____

Read the selection. Then answer the questions that follow.

Caitlin's Science Fair Project

Science was Caitlin's favorite subject, so naturally she was excited about the Science   13
Fair. For her project, Caitlin wanted to find out if noise and other distractions made it   29
harder to do homework.   33

To find out, she read from her social studies book while other things were going   48
on around her. She read in the same room where her brother was watching a television   64
program. She read while listening to her favorite music group. She read in a quiet room.   80
Then she read in a room crowded with family members talking to one another. She also   96
read on the school bus on her way to school.   106

She read from the same book each time, but she didn't read the same pages she had   123
read before. She read for the same length of time in each situation. Then she recorded   139
the number of pages she was able to read. Finally, Caitlin made this poster to take to the   157
Science Fair.   159

DO DISTRACTIONS MAKE IT HARD TO DO HOMEWORK?			
What Was Happening	**Pages Read**	**Number of Minutes**	**Reading Speed**
Television on	2	30	4 pages per hour
Jet Girls on stereo	8	30	16 pages per hour
Quiet room	7	30	14 pages per hour
Noisy room	5	30	11 pages per hour
On school bus	4	20	12 pages per hour

Conclusion Some kinds of distractions do make it hard to think.

Turn the page.

Answer the questions below.

1 **What happened that caused Caitlin to get excited?**

   A She loved school, and she could spend more time doing homework.

   B She loved her family, and she found she would be at home with them.

   C She loved social studies, and she could read her favorite textbook.

   (D) She loved science, and she learned she could be in the Science Fair.

2 **Why did Caitlin choose to read while her brother was watching television?**

   F She wanted to test whether she could do two things at once.

   G She did not want to miss her favorite TV show.

   (H) She wanted to see how distracting the program would be.

   J She was bored with her social studies textbook.

3 **For what reason did Caitlin read different pages each time?**

   (A) The information would continue to be new to her.

   B She could get her homework all done.

   C The information did not make sense the first time.

   D She could finish up the book much faster.

4 **Why did Caitlin read her social studies book instead of one of her favorite stories or a magazine?**

She wanted to know if noise made it harder to do homework, not just harder to read.

5 **Where was the best place for Caitlin to do her homework? Use information from the poster to explain your answer.**

The best place for Caitlin to do her homework was in her room with her favorite music playing because that was when she read the fastest.

Common Core State Standards

Questions 1–5: **Literature 1.** Refer to details and examples in a text when explaining what the text says explicitly and when drawing inferences from the text. **Literature 3.** Describe in depth a character, setting, or event in a story or drama, drawing on specific details in a text (e.g., a character's thoughts, words, or actions).

- -

84

Name _____

Read the selection. Then answer the questions that follow.

The Slow Sloth

In a forest of Central or South America, a sloth hangs in the trees. It hooks its huge, curved claws over a tree branch, where it hangs upside-down for several days at a time. The long legs of the sloth need to be strong to support its weight. Tiny plants called algae grow in its hair, giving the animal a greenish color. This helps the sloth hide from its enemies.

Sloth means "laziness." It moves slowly whenever it moves at all. The sloth rarely climbs down from the trees. Since it eats mainly leaves and small branches, food is all around. On the ground, its huge claws make walking difficult. So it "hangs out" in the trees most of the time, eating and sleeping.

18
34
51
68
70
84
100
116
124

Turn the page.

Answer the questions below.

1 **Which statement from the selection is a generalization about sloths?**

   A It hooks its huge, curved claws over a tree branch.

   B Tiny plants called algae grow in its hair.

   C The sloth's name means "laziness."

   (D) So it "hangs out" in the trees most of the time.

2 **What conclusion can you draw from the selection?**

   F The sloth often eats the larger tree branches.

   (G) The sloth does not need to walk to stay healthy.

   H The sloth gets dizzy hanging upside-down.

   J The sloth cleans the algae from its hair every day.

3 **Which of the following is a valid generalization?**

   (A) Sloths are well suited for life in trees.

   B Sloths are always lazy.

   C Sloths are impossible to find.

   D Sloths never leave the trees.

4 **Write two generalizations that can be made about the sloth to justify its name.**

   Possible responses: The sloth moves slowly whenever it moves. It seldom comes down from the trees.

Common Core State Standards

Questions 1–4: **Informational Text 1.** Refer to details and examples in a text when explaining what the text says explicitly and when drawing inferences from the text. **Informational Text 3.** Explain events, procedures, ideas, or concepts in a historical, scientific, or technical text, including what happened and why, based on specific information in the text.

Name _____

Read the selection. Then answer the questions that follow.

Cities in the Sea

Coral reefs are like great cities in the sea. Millions of creatures live in them. They	16
always lie in warm, clear ocean water. This is because the corals that build them need	32
warmth and sunlight to live.	37
These creatures are cousins of the jellyfish. They eat tiny plants and animals that	51
float in the water. They are shaped like short tubes and grow one on top of another.	68
They pile up, like apartment buildings for fish. Over time, some die and others grow on	84
their bones. Fish and other sea creatures add to the pile. Sand fills the spaces between	100
them. In this way, over many years, reefs are made. Some are thousands of years old and	117
cover many miles.	120
Fish, sea snakes, and other sea animals move in. In fact, the area becomes crowded	135
with life, just like a city. These city dwellers find holes that offer safety from their	151
enemies. They eat the tiny plants and animals that drift in the water. Many more eat each	168
other.	169
People eat the animals that live there too. We also make medicines from some of	184
them. Many people take vacations near reefs so they can dive around them. They enjoy	199
seeing the beautiful creatures that live and hunt there. However, we must take care of	214
these cities in the sea. Pollution, boating, fishing, and change in climate can all harm the	230
corals.	231

Turn the page.

Answer the questions below.

1 What clue word tells you that the following sentence is a generalization?

"Pollution, boating, fishing, and change in climate can all harm the corals."

A and

B change

C can

(D) all

2 What sentence from the selection is not a generalization?

F They always lie in warm, clear ocean water.

(G) Sand fills the spaces between them.

H Some are thousands of years old.

J Many people take vacations near reefs.

3 A good way to help the coral reefs would be to

(A) avoid throwing litter in the waters.

B drive more boats in around them.

C expand the fishing being done nearby.

D stop teaching people about them.

4 What valid generalization can readers make about coral reefs?

F Coral reefs are found in all warm water.

(G) People find many uses for coral reefs.

H Most of the world's fish live in coral reefs.

J Few coral reefs are left in the world.

5 What generalizations does the author make about cities?

That cities are crowded with life, and millions of people

live there.

Common Core State Standards

Questions 1–5: Informational Text 1. Refer to details and examples in a text when explaining what the text says explicitly and when drawing inferences from the text. Informational Text 3. Explain events, procedures, ideas, or concepts in a historical, scientific, or technical text, including what happened and why, based on specific information in the text.

Read the selection. Then answer the questions that follow.

Arctic Tundra

What Is It?	3

Arctic tundra is mostly flat land in areas that are too cold for trees to grow. Most | 20

of the world's tundra is near the Arctic Circle. In these areas, soil beneath the top layer | 37

stays frozen all the time. This frozen soil is called permafrost. | 48

Temperatures stay below freezing for most of the year. Summers are always short, | 61

and very little rain or snow falls. Water that does fall does not drain away, because | 77

the land is flat and mostly frozen. This means that when the weather warms up in the | 94

summer, much of the land turns into a muddy swamp. | 104

Wildlife | 105

Mosquitoes love swamps, and in the summer months the air is thick with them. | 119

Some birds nest in the bushes in summer and then fly south when the long winter sets | 136

in. Reindeer and other grazing animals eat low-growing plants. A few kinds | 148

of hares and rabbits do too. In turn, foxes, wolves, and snowy owls eat these animals. | 164

Compared with other places, the tundra is home to very few plants and animals. The | 179

climate is just too hard. | 184

People | 185

It doesn't sound like a great place to live, does it? The truth is, the arctic tundra is | 203

beautiful in its way. Some people do choose to live there. For a few groups in the United | 221

States and in Russia, this cold, lonely, and beautiful place is home. | 233

Turn the page.

Answer the questions below.

1 What clue word tells you that the following sentence is a generalization?

"Most of the world's tundra is inside the Arctic Circle."

(A) most

B world's

C is

D inside

2 Which of these sentences from the selection is not a generalization?

(F) This frozen soil is called permafrost.

G Summers are always short.

H Mosquitoes love swamps.

J Temperatures stay below freezing for most of the year.

3 Which of these is a valid generalization about the arctic tundra?

A Most animals that live there are meat-eaters.

(B) Winters are always long and cold.

C It never snows there.

D Snowy owls find plenty of food there.

4 Give two generalizations from the selection that support the following statement.

The arctic tundra doesn't sound like a great place to live.

Possible responses: Temperatures stay below freezing for most of the year. Summers are short. The land is swampy in the summer, and the air is full of mosquitoes.

5 If you were visiting the arctic tundra in the summer, what three things would be good to bring along? Support your answer with facts from the selection.

Answers may vary. Possible response: One would be bug spray, because a lot of mosquitoes are there in summer. Another would be good boots, because the land turns into a muddy mess. Finally, drinking water would be a good idea, because there is almost no rain and the swamps are all muddy and buggy.

Common Core State Standards

Questions 1–5: Informational Text 1. Refer to details and examples in a text when explaining what the text says explicitly and when drawing inferences from the text. **Informational Text 3.** Explain events, procedures, ideas, or concepts in a historical, scientific, or technical text, including what happened and why, based on specific information in the text.

Name _____

Read the selection. Then answer the questions that follow.

Gathering Leaves

Alyssa's class was collecting autumn leaves for the bulletin board. When Alyssa	12
went to the park to gather some, she met a boy from her class. "Hey, Lucas," said	29
Alyssa.	30
"Hey," said Lucas, as he dropped a flawless, star-shaped leaf into a paper sack.	44
"That's a nice one," said Alyssa. She scooped up an armful of leaves from a pile	60
beside the path and stuffed them into her sack.	69
"It's from a sycamore tree," answered Lucas. He inspected a red, heart-shaped leaf	82
for a moment before discarding it.	88
Alyssa stared. The leaf was as intensely red as a valentine, so bright she couldn't	103
stop looking at it. The sycamore leaves were fine, but this tiny red one was a treasure.	120
She picked it up and dropped it into her sack.	130
As Lucas chose a second perfect sycamore leaf, Alyssa kicked noisily through a drift	144
and scooped another armful.	148

Turn the page.

Answer the questions below.

1 To what did the author compare the small red leaf?

   A a star

   B a person

   C a fish

   (D) a valentine

2 For what reason did Alyssa stare?

   F She thought that Lucas was being silly.

   G She thought she found the perfect sycamore leaf.

   (H) She thought the red leaf was very special.

   J She thought she was going to drop all her leaves.

3 How was Alyssa's method of gathering leaves different from Lucas's?

   A Alyssa took her time.

   B Alyssa picked up only red ones.

   (C) Alyssa gathered them by the armful.

   D Alyssa knew the names of the trees.

4 Describe one way that Lucas and Alyssa were different and one way that they were alike.

Answers may vary. Possible responses: Lucas knew more about leaves than Alyssa did. He was more careful in choosing leaves. She liked playing with the leaves more than selecting them. They both liked autumn leaves. They are both in the same class.

Common Core State Standards

Question 1: Literature 1. Refer to details and examples in a text when explaining what the text says explicitly and when drawing inferences from the text.
Questions 2–4: Literature 3. Describe in depth a character, setting, or event in a story or drama, drawing on specific details in a text (e.g., a character's thoughts, words, or actions).

Name _____

Read the selection. Then answer the questions that follow.

The Poster

"The book says it's a white-crowned sparrow," said Andrew. "You can tell because the white stripes on its head look like a crown." | 13 / 23

"Hello, Your Majesty," Habib joked as he sketched in the stripes on the bird he was drawing. As he drew, he glanced back and forth from the bird to his sketchbook. When the drawing was done, he ripped out the page and handed it to Andrew, who made a note on a card: "White-crowned sparrow, seen April 9 in Habib's yard." | 39 / 55 / 72 / 84

"That's it," said Andrew with satisfaction. "That's the last one." | 94

They took the drawing inside, and Habib glued it to the last empty spot on their poster. The science project was finished. They had found twenty-eight kinds of birds and looked each one up in Andrew's book *Birds of North America*. Andrew had written a note card for each bird, and Habib had put together the poster. | 110 / 123 / 138 / 151

The poster had a drawing or photograph for every bird. Andrew liked taking photographs because they showed exactly what the bird looked like. Habib liked drawing. It took longer but made him feel that he knew more about the bird, after looking at it for so long. So half the birds were pictured in photos and the other half in drawings. | 164 / 176 / 192 / 211 / 212

Tomorrow in school they would present their poster to the class and use the note cards to tell about the birds. Habib could hardly wait! | 227 / 237

Turn the page.

Answer the questions below.

1 In the second paragraph, to what did Habib compare the white-crowned sparrow?

   A a tiger's stripes

   B a painting

   (C) a king or queen

   D another bird

2 What is one way Habib's pictures were different from Andrew's?

   F They looked more like birds.

   (G) They took longer to make.

   H They were more colorful.

   J They were smaller.

3 What is probably one reason that Andrew and Habib were friends?

   A They had the same skills and talents.

   B Both liked to make jokes and kid around.

   C They grew up next door to each other.

   (D) They were interested in the same things.

4 Why do you think Habib glanced back and forth from the bird to his sketchbook?

   (F) to draw the details of the bird's appearance correctly

   G to keep the bird from moving to a different branch

   H to check in the guide book to know which bird it was

   J to act as if he were a bird looking for food to eat

5 Do you think the work was divided fairly? Use details from the selection to explain your answer.

   Yes, the work was fairly divided. Each boy made half the pictures and did one other job.

Common Core State Standards

Questions 1, 5: Literature 1. Refer to details and examples in a text when explaining what the text says explicitly and when drawing inferences from the text. **Questions 2–4: Literature 3.** Describe in depth a character, setting, or event in a story or drama, drawing on specific details in a text (e.g., a character's thoughts, words, or actions).

Name _____

Read the selection. Then answer the questions that follow.

A Change of Heart

Richard gazed out the classroom windows and didn't like what he saw. The trees | 14

along the playing field were covered in white blossoms, as they had been all week. For | 30

Richard, they were like clouds of poison. He was allergic to those flowers. He knew that | 45

if he went outside today, his eyes would swell and his nose would run. He would feel as | 62

if he couldn't breathe. He knew, because it had happened to him on Monday, and since | 78

that day he had not been able to go out on the field. | 93

At lunch Mr. Hunter told him, "Ms. Gomez is expecting you in the library, Richard. | 108

Have fun." Richard nodded sadly. He hoped those trees would stop blooming soon so | 122

he could go out with the other kids. He was tired of sitting in the library while everyone | 140

else played outside. | 143

Then Luci said, "I'll go with you, if that's OK." Luci was on crutches because she | 159

had hurt her foot in a basketball game. | 167

"Do you have to go to the library too?" asked Richard, thinking she couldn't go out | 183

because of her injury. | 187

Luci shrugged. "I'd rather go to the library. We'll have all the books to ourselves. | 202

There's one about spiders I've been wanting to read, but someone else always gets it | 217

first." | 218

Richard knew the book she meant, because everyone had been talking about it. In | 232

fact, he'd been wanting to read it too. Maybe the library wasn't so bad after all. | 248

Turn the page.

Answer the questions below.

1 In the simile in the first paragraph, what two things does the author compare?

   A   cotton and clouds

   B   flowers and milk

   C   clouds and poison

   (**D**) poison and flowers

2 What did Luci and Richard have in common?

   F   Neither one liked to read.

   (**G**) Neither one could play outside.

   H   Neither one was allergic to spring flowers.

   J   Neither one played basketball.

3 How was Luci's attitude different from Richard's?

   A   She wanted to go outside.

   B   She wanted to be alone.

   (**C**) She was glad to go to the library.

   D   She didn't like what she saw out the window.

4 In what way were Richard's feelings at the end of the story different from his feelings at the beginning?

He was feeling less sorry for himself at the end,

more interested in things he could do than in things

he couldn't do.

5 What happened to cause Richard to think differently about going to the library?

Luci reminded him about a book he'd been wanting

to read.

Common Core State Standards

Question 1: Literature 1. Refer to details and examples in a text when explaining what the text says explicitly and when drawing inferences from the text.
Questions 2–5: Literature 3. Describe in depth a character, setting, or event in a story or drama, drawing on specific details in a text (e.g., a character's thoughts, words, or actions).

Name _____

Read the selection. Then answer the questions that follow.

Clocks

Noah inserted the clock key into a hole in the clock face and turned it three times. | 17

The clock chimed with a loud *bong,* as it did every hour and every time Noah wound it. | 35

His great aunt had carried it when she moved from Russia to the United States decades | 51

before. The clock was older than Noah, older even than his parents. It had to be wound | 68

every morning or it would stop, and winding it was Noah's responsibility. | 80

He thought about asking his mother if he could move the clock into his room, | 95

although he knew it would wake him every time it chimed. "Most of my friends have | 111

clocks in their rooms," he hinted. | 117

"This isn't the sort of clock to have in your room," his mother answered. "Most | 132

modern clocks don't chime, and they don't need to be wound." | 143

Noah traced the carved wood with his fingers. He was not especially impressed | 156

with modern clocks. | 159

Turn the page.

Answer the questions below.

1 How was the old clock different from most modern clocks?

(A) It had to be wound.

B It didn't keep time as well.

C It came from another country.

D It was much smaller.

2 In what way were Noah and his great aunt alike?

F Both of them once lived in Russia.

(G) Both wanted to keep the older clock with them.

H Neither one liked modern clocks.

J Neither one remembered to wind the clock.

3 Which statement from the story is a generalization?

A It was older than Noah, even older than his parents.

B Winding it was Noah's responsibility.

(C) Most of my friends have clocks in their rooms.

D Noah traced the carved wood with his fingers.

4 Would you like a clock like Noah's better than a modern clock? Explain your answer.

Answers may vary. Possible responses: Yes, I would like a clock that chimed. No, I wouldn't like to wind a clock every day.

Common Core State Standards

Questions 1, 3, 4: Literature 1. Refer to details and examples in a text when explaining what the text says explicitly and when drawing inferences from the text. Question 2: Literature 3. Describe in depth a character, setting, or event in a story or drama, drawing on specific details in a text (e.g., a character's thoughts, words, or actions).

Name _____

Read the selection. Then answer the questions that follow.

Making a Decision

Dear Sis,

How is college? We have all missed you since you moved away from home.

Our big news is that we're going to get a dog. Mom and Dad drove us to the animal shelter yesterday to choose one. Miguel liked a little white dog. Her name is Cotton. She only weighs six pounds, even though she is fully grown. Mom says she is a "lap dog." That means she is a good size for Miguel to hold in his lap. She is too small to spend much time outside, though. Dad says she would be a good watchdog because she barked the whole time we were at the shelter.

My favorite is a puppy named Rex. Rex is already larger than the white dog, even though he's only three months old. He has big floppy ears and thick brown fur. His feet are almost like pancakes. Dad says he'll weigh forty or fifty pounds when he's fully grown. That's OK with me. I want a big dog that I can take running with me in the park.

Most of the dogs we saw yesterday were friendly. I'd be happy to bring any of them home. The real problem is making a decision. What do you think? Should we adopt a sweet little lap dog or a big dog like Rex? Maybe we should get them both!

Anyway, when you come home for summer break you'll meet our new four-footed family member!

Your sister,

Cristina

2
16
35
50
67
87
102
111
127
144
159
178
179
196
212
228
241
243
245
246

Turn the page.

Answer the questions below.

1 **How are Cotton and Rex alike?**

   A Both make good lap dogs.

   (B) Both are at the animal shelter.

   C Both have large ears and feet.

   D Both weigh forty or fifty pounds.

2 **Why are Rex's feet compared to pancakes in the third paragraph?**

   (F) to show the size of his feet

   G to imply that his feet are messy

   H because they both are warm

   J to show the color of his feet

3 **Which statement from the letter is a generalization?**

   A Mom and Dad drove us to the animal shelter yesterday to choose one.

   B My favorite is a puppy named Rex.

   (C) Most of the dogs we saw yesterday were friendly.

   D Maybe we should get them both!

4 **What answer best completes this chart comparing the two dogs?**

Cotton	Rex
6 pounds	40 or 50 pounds
lap dog	outdoor dog
?	still a puppy

   F barks a lot

   (G) fully grown

   H white coat

   J long hair

5 **How are Cristina and Miguel alike, and how are they different? Give at least one example of each.**

Answers may vary. Possible responses: Cristina and Miguel both want a dog. Cristina seems to be older and bigger than Miguel since she wants a bigger dog.

Common Core State Standards

Questions 1, 2, 5: Literature 3. Describe in depth a character, setting, or event in a story or drama, drawing on specific details in a text (e.g., a character's thoughts, words, or actions). Questions 3, 4: Literature 1. Refer to details and examples in a text when explaining what the text says explicitly and when drawing inferences from the text.

100

Name _____

Read the selection. Then answer the questions that follow.

A Faster Way to Send Messages

If you want to give a message to a friend in another city, you could make a   17
telephone call. If you have a computer, you could send an e-mail.   29

In the early 1800s, there were no computers, and Alexander Graham Bell had not   43
yet invented the telephone. Most people wrote letters, but mail was slower than it is 58
today. Mail traveled by boat or horseback, so a letter could take a very long time to go 76
from one city to another.   81

A man named Samuel Morse thought that people should have a faster way to send   96
messages. Morse knew that some scientists had been working to solve this problem,   109
and he began experimenting too. He had heard about machines that sent controlled   122
bursts of electricity over wires. He built a better machine than the other scientists. His 137
machine—the telegraph—sent short and long bursts of electricity over very long wires. 151

Next, Morse's partner Alfred Vail designed a code for sending messages. In his   164
code, the short and long bursts of energy were combined in different ways. Each   178
combination stood for a letter of the alphabet. For example, a short and a long burst 194
stood for the letter *A*. One long and three short bursts stood for the letter *B*. With Morse 212
code, people could send messages over long distances in a short period of time.   226

There were many changes in communication after Morse's invention. The telegraph   237
caught on, and wires were strung from city to city. People were informed about   251
important news more quickly than ever before. Businesspeople used the telegraph   262
to buy and sell products. People could send messages across the country in minutes,   276
instead of months.   279

Turn the page.

Answer the questions below.

1 What was one difference between the telegraph and mail in the early 1800s?

    A It cost more to send a letter than to use a telegraph.

    B There were more telegraph offices than post offices.

    (C) The telegraph was faster than the mail.

    D The telegraph traveled by boat while a letter traveled by horseback.

2 What did Alexander Graham Bell and Samuel Morse have in common?

    F Both worked on the first telegraph.

    (G) Both invented ways to send messages.

    H Both were born in the early 1800s.

    J Both started out working for the post office.

3 What statement from the selection is a generalization?

    A If you have a computer, you could send an e-mail.

    (B) Most people wrote letters, but mail was slower than it is today.

    C Morse knew that some scientists had been trying to solve this problem.

    D One long and three short bursts stood for the letter *B*.

4 How would you communicate with a friend in another city, and how would that be different from using a telegraph?

Answers may vary. Possible responses: I would use the telephone. I don't need to use a code. Instead, I speak to my friend and can hear my friend's voice.

5 In what way was the invention of the telegraph like the invention of the computer?

Both let messages be sent faster than before.

Common Core State Standards

Questions 1, 2, 4, 5: **Informational Text 3.** Explain events, procedures, ideas, or concepts in a historical, scientific, or technical text, including what happened and why, based on specific information in the text. **Question 3: Informational Text 1.** Refer to details and examples in a text when explaining what the text says explicitly and when drawing inferences from the text.

Read the selection. Then answer the questions that follow.

From the Vine to the Box

People have turned grapes into raisins for thousands of years, but have you ever | 14
wondered how? | 16

First, workers pick grapes from their vines, and then they spread them on wooden | 30
trays that are set between the vines. The fruit wrinkles and dries under the searing sun | 46
for two weeks, after which it gets stacked in enormous bins to dry more. Raisins have | 62
one-fourth the water of grapes, and four and a half pounds of grapes will yield one | 78
pound of raisins. | 81

Next, the raisins journey to packing houses where workers sort them by quality and | 95
size. They put the raisins through a machine that squeezes out the seeds. | 108

Finally, the raisins are put into boxes and shipped by train and truck. People | 122
everywhere enjoy snacking on them. | 127

Turn the page.

Answer the questions below.

1 **What happens right *after* the grapes are picked?**

A The grapes journey to packing houses.

B The grapes are put into boxes.

(C) Workers spread the grapes on trays.

D Workers put the grapes into enormous bins.

2 **Which words show that one step leads to the next?**

F grapes, raisins, set, stacked

(G) first, then, next, finally

H wondered, pick, spread, dry

J vines, trays, bins, boxes

3 **Which statement from the selection shows a step in the process?**

A People have turned grapes into raisins for thousands of years.

(B) The fruit wrinkles and dries under the sun for two weeks.

C Four-and-a-half pounds of grapes will yield one pound of raisins.

D Raisins have one-fourth of the water of grapes.

4 **Tell a sentence from the selection that is a generalization about raisins.**

Possible response: People everywhere enjoy snacking on them.

_____

_____

_____

_____

_____

_____

_____

Common Core State Standards

Questions 1–4: Informational Text 3. Explain events, procedures, ideas, or concepts in a historical, scientific, or technical text, including what happened and why, based on specific information in the text.

Name _____

Read the selection. Then answer the questions that follow.

How to Grow Cantaloupe

Nothing tastes more delicious than a just-picked cantaloupe you have grown	11
yourself. All you need is good soil, healthy seeds, plenty of water, and a three-month	26
stretch of hot sun.	30
First, pick the perfect spot that has full sun and rich soil. Build a hill of soil about	48
three feet around and two feet high. Set the hills four to six feet apart.	63
Next, buy a package of high-quality cantaloupe seeds. Plant them after the last frost	77
when the soil begins to warm. Plant four to six seeds per hill, one-half to one inch deep.	95
In several days, the cantaloupe seeds will sprout. On each hill, select the three or	110
four healthiest ones. Pluck out the others. Then just keep the plants moist and watch	125
them take off.	128
Because cantaloupe plants require a lot of water, give them a good soaking once or	143
twice a week. As they grow, arrange them to keep the vines from crossing each other.	159
Cantaloupes do not like to be cold, and frost will quickly kill them. If frost is	175
predicted, cover your plants.	179
A cantaloupe is ripe when the stem begins to dry and the end of the cantaloupe is	196
soft when pressed. A melon is too ripe when it is soft all over. Once it is picked, it will	216
last about a week.	220
It takes seventy to ninety days to grow a cantaloupe, but a fresh one is well worth	237
the wait.	239

Turn the page.

Answer the questions below.

1 What is the *first* step to growing cantaloupe?

  A Plant four to six seeds per hill.

  B Test the soil for its health.

  C Give the plants lots of water.

  (D) Pick a growing spot.

2 What is the *last* step to growing a cantaloupe?

  F Water the cantaloupe plants.

  G Pick the healthiest cantaloupe plants.

  (H) Make sure the cantaloupe is ripe.

  J Buy cantaloupe seeds.

3 Which two steps happen at the same time?

  A planting seeds and covering in case of frost

  (B) watering plants and keeping vines from crossing

  C buying seeds and plucking the least healthy plants

  D building hills and planting seeds

4 Which phrase from the passage describes a step that happens over many days?

  F "four to six feet apart"

  (G) "watch them take off"

  H "frost will quickly kill them"

  J "the end of the cantaloupe is soft"

5 What generalization can be made about cantaloupes based on the selection?

<u>**Possible response: Whenever cantaloupes become soft all**</u>

<u>**over, they are too ripe.**</u>

_____

_____

_____

_____

Common Core State Standards

Questions 1–5: Informational Text 3. Explain events, procedures, ideas, or concepts in a historical, scientific, or technical text, including what happened and why, based on specific information in the text.

Read the selection. Then answer the questions that follow.

Maggie's Dill Beans

4 to 5 pounds freshly picked green beans	8
8 to 16 heads fresh dill	14
8 cloves garlic	17
4 cups white vinegar	21
4 cups water	24
1/3 cup salt	27

When the beans take their turn in the garden, they all ripen at once, so we eat them | 45

every day in July and August. This recipe offers a convenient and delicious way to | 60

savor the taste of green beans all year. | 68

First, pick as many beans as possible, and then trim or snap off the ends. Wash | 84

them well under cold running water and cut them into 4-inch lengths. | 96

Next, combine the vinegar, water, and salt in a pot. While the water rises to a boil | 113

over high heat, arrange eight clean pint jars on the table or counter. | 126

While the vinegar is boiling, place 2 generous heads of dill and 2 cloves of garlic | 142

in each jar. Then pack green beans tightly into each jar, arranging as many as possible, | 158

with a half inch of space remaining at the top of each jar. | 171

Now slowly and carefully pour the steaming hot vinegar mixture into each jar. Use | 185

a clean chopstick or long spoon to stir out any air bubbles. Gently wipe the jar tops | 202

with a clean cloth and screw the lids on tightly. | 212

Finally, boil the jars in water for 10 minutes. Let them sit until each one is sealed. | 229

These dill beans will last for months, and they will remind you of summer all year. | 245

Turn the page.

Answer the questions below.

1 Which step happens *last* when making dill beans?

   A Pack the beans into the jars.

   (B) Boil the jars for 10 minutes.

   C Pour the hot vinegar mixture into the jars.

   D Put dill and garlic in the jars.

2 What is the *first* step in making dill beans?

   F putting the beans into jars

   G washing the beans

   H cutting the beans

   (J) picking the beans

3 Which two steps happen at the same time?

   (A) boiling the vinegar and packing the jars

   B washing the beans and cutting them into 4-inch pieces

   C wiping the jar tops and packing the garlic

   D pouring the vinegar and screwing on the jar lids

4 What do you do *right after* you pour the vinegar into the jars?

   F screw on the lids

   (G) stir out any bubbles

   H add the green beans

   J clean off the tops

5 What generalization can you make about green beans?

Answers may vary. Possible response: In the garden, all the green beans seem to ripen at the same time.

Common Core State Standards

Questions 1–5: **Informational Text 3.** Explain events, procedures, ideas, or concepts in a historical, scientific, or technical text, including what happened and why, based on specific information in the text.

Name _____

Read the selection. Then answer the questions that follow.

The Liberty Bell

The colony of Pennsylvania ordered the Liberty Bell in 1751 and had it shipped | 14

from England. On the day it was hung, it cracked. The broken bell was melted down, | 30

and the same metal was used to make a new one. | 41

For most Americans, the Liberty Bell is a symbol of freedom. Carved on it are the | 57

words "Proclaim Liberty throughout all the land." It rang to call people together the | 71

first time the Declaration of Independence was read. For many years after that, the bell | 86

rang every Fourth of July. But soon another crack began to develop. By Washington's | 100

birthday in 1846 the crack had grown so wide that the bell could no longer be rung. | 117

3 FEET

2 FEET

1 FOOT

In the mid-1800s, a crack appeared in the Liberty Bell. For this reason, it is no longer rung. Cracked and silent, the bell is still a symbol of freedom. Today it hangs in Philadelphia, Pennsylvania.

Turn the page.

Answer the questions below.

1 **Where is the Liberty Bell now?**

   A Washington, D.C.

   B London, England

   (C) Philadelphia, Pennsylvania

   D Independence, Missouri

2 **The picture of the Liberty Bell tells you that it is about**

   F one foot high.

   G two feet high.

   (H) three feet high.

   J four feet high.

3 **Which statement about the Liberty Bell is supported by its picture?**

   A It is too loud.

   (B) It is cracked.

   C It was melted down.

   D It came from England.

4 **How are the first and second Liberty Bells the same?**

Possible response: They were both made from the same metal, and they both cracked.

Common Core State Standards

Questions 1, 4: Informational Text 1. Refer to details and examples in a text when explaining what the text says explicitly and when drawing inferences from the text. **Questions 2, 3: Informational Text 7.** Interpret information presented visually, orally, or quantitatively (e.g., in charts, graphs, diagrams, time lines, animations, or interactive elements on Web pages) and explain how the information contributes to an understanding of the text in which it appears.

Name _____

Read the selection. Then answer the questions that follow.

The Great Sahara

The great Sahara was not always a desert. A few thousand years ago, farmers were   15

able to grow crops there. The region received more rainfall then, and the soil was rich.   31

Then, over many years, the climate changed. Rain stopped falling, the soil became dry,   45

and the farmers left.   49

The Sahara's climate is now very dry. In some places, no rain falls for years at a   66

time. As you might expect, days are often blisteringly hot. It may surprise you to learn   82

that nights in the desert can be freezing cold.   91

Most people think of this desert as having three parts: the rocky western part, the   106

mountains in the middle, and the eastern part, which is the driest. The eastern area is   122

what many people think of when they think of desert. Great hills of sand rise hundreds   138

of feet in the air. These rolling dunes stretch as far as the eye can see.   154

Humans have lived on the edges of the desert for thousands of years. After the   169

Arabs brought camels to the area, people finally had an animal that could carry them   184

across the desert. But most traders still prefer to earn their livings elsewhere. In general,   199

the Sahara is a harsh and unwelcoming place to living things.   210

?

The Sahara covers much of northern Africa, stretching from the Atlantic Ocean to the Red Sea.

Turn the page.

Answer the questions below.

1 How has the Sahara changed from thousands of years ago to today?

   A The Sahara used to have sand hills; now it is all flat.

   B The Sahara used to be very dry; now it gets some rain.

   C The Sahara used to be farm land; now it is desert.

   D The Sahara used to have hot days; now it has cold nights.

2 On the west, the border of the Sahara is the

   F Sea of Nasser.

   G Atlantic Ocean.

   H Pacific Ocean.

   J Red Sea.

3 According to the map, what river runs through the Sahara?

   A The Nile River

   B The Red River

   C The Tripoli River

   D The Mediterranean River

4 What is the best title for the map?

   F The Eastern Sahara

   G The Sahara in Modern Times

   H Ancient Farms in the Sahara

   J Mountain Trails of the Sahara

5 The map shows several African cities. Where are the cities in relation to the Sahara?

The cities seem to be around the outside edges of the desert.

Common Core State Standards

Question 1: Informational Text 1. Refer to details and examples in a text when explaining what the text says explicitly and when drawing inferences from the text. Questions 2–5: Informational Text 7. Interpret information presented visually, orally, or quantitatively (e.g., in charts, graphs, diagrams, time lines, animations, or interactive elements on Web pages) and explain how the information contributes to an understanding of the text in which it appears.

Name _____

Read the selection. Then answer the questions that follow.

One of the World's Oldest Toys

You slip the loop of string over your finger, and your hand curls around the toy. Your | 16
hand flips backward, and the yo-yo rolls down the string. It spins at the end of its string | 34
for a fraction of a second and then bounces back up to your hand. Once you start playing | 52
with a yo-yo, it's hard to stop. | 60

The word *yo-yo* comes from a country known as the Philippines. It means "come, | 74
come." Children there have been playing with this type of toy for hundreds of years, | 89
although they were not the first. Greek children have had yo-yos for thousands of years. | 104
It is one of the world's oldest toys. | 112

?
_____

Pedro Flores, a Filipino American, opens a yo-yo factory in Santa Barbara, California. Soon he opens two more factories. Flores also starts holding contests. To win, people have to keep their yo-yos spinning up and down for hours without stopping or making any mistakes. The contests draw big crowds. This is when the toy really becomes a hit in this country.

A new kind of yo-yo becomes popular. This one makes it easier to do tricks, even for beginners.

An ancient vase shows a child in Greece playing with a yo-yo 2,500 years ago.

500 B.C.   **1928**   **1960s**

1866
Two men, James L. Haven and Charles Hettrich, are issued the first U.S. patent on a toy similar to the yo-yo.

1930
Donald Duncan buys Flores's corporation. Duncan sells even more yo-yos than Flores had. When people think of yo-yos, they think of Duncan.

Turn the page.

Answer the questions below.

1 Which fact from the selection does the timeline support?

   A The word *yo-yo* comes from the Philippines.

   B Philippine children have had yo-yos for hundreds of years.

   (C) Greek children had yo-yos thousands of years ago.

   D The word *yo-yo* means "come, come" in the Philippines.

2 What happened in the 1960s, according to the time line?

   F Hettrich and Haven received a patent on the yo-yo.

   G Factories started to mass-produce yo-yos.

   H Yo-yo contests became popular.

   (J) A new type of yo-yo made it easier to do tricks.

3 What would make the best title for the time line?

   A Types of Yo-Yos

   B How to Use a Yo-Yo

   C How a Yo-Yo Is Made

   (D) The History of Yo-Yos

4 Tell one way that Pedro Flores and Donald Duncan were alike. Then, tell one way that these two men were different.

Possible response: Alike: Both men owned the same yo-yo corporation. Different: Duncan sold more yo-yos than Flores.

5 According to the time line, who was Pedro Flores and why was he important?

Pedro Flores owned yo-yo factories. He made the toy popular in this country by holding contests, which drew big crowds.

Common Core State Standards

Questions 1–3, 5: **Informational Text 7.** Interpret information presented visually, orally, or quantitatively (e.g., in charts, graphs, diagrams, time lines, animations, or interactive elements on Web pages) and explain how the information contributes to an understanding of the text in which it appears.
Question 4: **Informational Text 1.** Refer to details and examples in a text when explaining what the text says explicitly and when drawing inferences from the text.

Read the selection. Then answer the questions that follow.

A Prickly Situation

Bart, the cowhand, sometimes walked in his sleep. His buddy, Simms, kept the	13
bunkhouse cleaned up so Bart would not stumble while sleepwalking. Then one day	26
they were on a roundup far from home and had to camp out in the hills.	42
Bart started snoring as soon as his head hit the bedroll. But he woke up at midnight,	59
standing in his flannel pajamas in the middle of a thicket of prickly pear cactus.	74
Amazingly, there was not a scratch on him!	82
He shouted for help, and Simms hurried out to see what all the ruckus was about.	98
"How did you get in there without getting poked?" he asked.	109
Bart grumbled, "I don't know—I was sleeping! How do you reckon I can get out of	126
here?"	127
Simms said, "Maybe you should go back to sleep."	136
So Bart curled up on the ground, and at sunup he awoke safe and sound in his own	154
bedroll.	155

Turn the page.

Answer the questions below.

1 **What was Bart's main problem in the story?**

   A The bunkhouse was too clean.

   B Simms was never around when Bart needed him.

   C He was afraid of sleeping outside.

   (D) He sleepwalked into a cactus patch.

2 **What did Bart do when he woke up in the cactus patch?**

   (F) He called Simms.

   G He stepped over the cactus.

   H He looked for the trail.

   J He told Simms to stop shouting.

3 **What *best* describes how Simms acts toward Bart?**

   A Teasing and tough

   B Careless and loud

   C Awake and worried

   (D) Helpful and kind

4 **How were Bart and Simms alike, and how were they different?**

They were both cowhands, but Bart had a sleepwalking

problem and Simms did not.

Common Core State Standards

Questions 1–4: Literature 3. Describe in depth a character, setting, or event in a story or drama, drawing on specific details in a text (e.g., a character's thoughts, words, or actions).

Name _____

Read the selection. Then answer the questions that follow.

The Flag

When Mr. Brown announced that they would make a class flag, no one suspected	14
that it would turn out to be so difficult. Ann said she knew exactly what it should look	32
like: white stars on a purple background. Some of the others laughed. That was the first	48
clue that it might not be easy to find an idea the whole class would like.	64
All the classes were making flags. Mr. Brown reminded his students that each flag	78
was supposed to tell something about the students in the class. A purple flag with white	94
stars would say nothing about the students in Mr. Brown's class.	105
Luis suggested, "Katie and I play soccer, and so does Tran. How about a green	120
background with a soccer ball on it?"	127
"What about the rest of the class?" Mr. Brown reminded him. "Max plays baseball,	141
Rachel plays basketball, and some students aren't interested in sports."	151
"Everyone likes music, don't they?" offered Rachel. "How about a black musical	163
note on a white background?"	168
Tran shook his head. "I like music, but I don't think a musical note tells anything	184
about me."	186
Katie's eyes were thoughtful as she said, "There are nineteen of us in this class."	201
"So?" asked Mario. "You think we should put a number on our flag?"	214
"No," said Katie. "The main thing we all have in common is that we are all	230
different. What if we put nineteen kids on the flag, with no two kids exactly the same?"	247
Katie's suggestion pleased everyone, but Luis still had one question. "What color	259
should the background be?"	263
"Brown, naturally!" replied Mr. Brown, with a comical grin.	272

Turn the page.

Answer the questions below.

1 What was the problem Mr. Brown's class had to solve?

  A how to choose colors for a class flag

  (B) how to make a flag that represented the whole class

  C how to agree on something when everyone had a different idea

  D how to make a decision when everyone wanted to talk at once

2 Which of the following was part of the rising action?

  (F) Ann suggested white stars on a purple background.

  G Katie's suggestion pleased everyone.

  H Mr. Brown knew what color the background should be.

  J Luis still had one question.

3 What was wrong with both Ann's and Luis's suggestions?

  A Neither suggested colors that everyone liked.

  B Neither showed a sport or a musical note.

  C Neither was an idea that would look good on a flag.

  (D) Neither said something about everyone in the class.

4 How did Katie's suggestion resolve the problem?

  F It showed both a soccer ball and a musical note.

  G It met with Mr. Brown's approval.

  (H) It showed something about the class.

  J It showed most of the class.

5 Describe how the students in Mr. Brown's class treat each other.

  Possible response: While they are all a little different, they speak up to each other in a nice way when they don't agree, and they work together thoughtfully to find a good group solution.

Common Core State Standards

Questions 1–5: Literature 3. Describe in depth a character, setting, or event in a story or drama, drawing on specific details in a text (e.g., a character's thoughts, words, or actions).

Name _____

Read the selection. Then answer the questions that follow.

Easy As Pie

The truck rattled to a stop beside a sign that read Downtown Bus. Mr. Aguilar	15
said, "Meet me back here at four o'clock." Will and his grandmother scrambled out,	29
slammed the door, and waved as Mr. Aguilar drove away.	39
Grandmother pulled a map out of her capacious handbag and pointed. "We'll take	52
this bus downtown and get off at the county courthouse. Easy as pie."	65
Will was excited about visiting the city and wanted to experience everything. He	78
was even excited about riding the bus. He lived with his grandmother in the small town	94
of Farrell, where a person could stroll from one end of town to the other in ten minutes.	112
When the bus arrived, they got in line behind a man with hair that spiked out in all	130
directions. He fed a dollar bill into a box beside the driver. Grandmother attempted to	145
stuff a folded-up dollar bill into the slot, which caused the driver to mutter something	160
under his breath. She unfolded the bill and it slipped right in.	172
Once they were seated, she kept glancing from her map to the window. "What's	186
wrong?" asked Will.	189
"These street names don't look familiar," worried Grandmother. "I'm afraid we've	200
taken the wrong bus."	204
Will studied the map and said, "I don't think you're looking at the right part of the	221
map. Aren't we really here?" He pointed.	228
Grandmother nodded sharply. "Smart boy. Now I wonder how we get this bus to	242
stop."	243
Will suddenly realized that his grandmother had never ridden a city bus either. They	257
were passing the courthouse! What should they do?	265
The spiky-haired man smiled from across the aisle. "This bus always stops at the	279
next corner," he said.	283
Will sighed with relief.	287
"Easy as pie," said Grandmother.	292

Turn the page.

Answer the questions below.

1 What was the first problem Will and Grandmother had?

A   getting on the wrong bus

(B) putting money in the box

C   getting off at the wrong stop

D   not knowing how to stop the bus

2 What event from the story is an example of rising action?

(F) Grandmother saying they might be on the wrong bus

G   Will being excited about his visit to the city

H   Grandmother and Will getting off the bus

J   Mr. Aguilar dropping them off at the bus stop

3 Why did Grandmother call Will a smart boy?

A   He had been sassy and quite disrespectful.

B   He asked the bus to stop at the county courthouse.

(C) He figured out where they were on the map.

D   He knew how to feed the dollar into the fare box.

4 How were Will's feelings at the beginning of the story different from his feelings at the end?

At first he was excited about having a new experience. At the end, he was just relieved to get where they wanted to go.

5 What was the resolution of the problem in this story?

A stranger told Will and his grandmother where the bus stopped.

4 Copyright © Pearson Education, Inc., or its affiliates. All Rights Reserved.

Common Core State Standards

Questions 1–5: **Literature 3.** Describe in depth a character, setting, or event in a story or drama, drawing on specific details in a text (e.g., a character's thoughts, words, or actions).

Name _____

Read the selection. Then answer the questions that follow.

Racing to the South Pole

    In 1911, two men and their teams raced to the South Pole. The South Pole, the | 16

southernmost point on the Earth, is a cold and empty place. The men were Captains | 31

Robert Scott from England and Roald Amundsen from Norway. | 40

    First, the men sailed ships to the Ross Sea. Their teams put food and tools in place | 57

along their routes to the South Pole. Then they set up base camp. The race was on! | 74

    Scott's team had ponies, dog sleds, and motor sledges while Amundsen's team | 86

had only dog sleds. Amundsen thought Scott would win because of his motor sledges. | 100

Scott's motors, however, broke down in the cold, and his ponies had trouble on the ice. | 116

Amundsen won the race! He reached the pole on December 15, 1911. Scott got there | 131

33 days later. | 134

Turn the page.

Answer the questions below.

1 What is probably the main reason the author wrote this selection?

(A) to tell readers about an event in history

B to explain to readers what the South Pole is like

C to persuade readers to try dog sled racing

D to teach readers where the South Pole is found

2 What is the *most likely* reason that the author included the following sentence, at the end of the second paragraph?

"The race was on!"

F to give facts about what kind of race it was

G to make clear to you how close the race was

H to describe the place where the race started

(J) to show that the start of the race was exciting

3 In the first paragraph, the author tells readers what the South Pole is like so that

A you want to go there and see it on your vacation.

B you wear the right kind of clothing when you visit.

(C) you understand how difficult a race would have been.

D you learn how different it is from England or Norway.

4 Based upon the map, describe how Scott and Amundsen's routes to the South Pole were different.

Possible responses: Scott and Amundsen traveled on different sides of the Ross Ice Shelf to get to the South Pole.

Common Core State Standards

Questions 1–3: Informational Text 8. Explain how an author uses reasons and evidence to support particular points in a text. Question 4: Informational Text 7. Interpret information presented visually, orally, or quantitatively (e.g., in charts, graphs, diagrams, time lines, animations, or interactive elements on Web pages) and explain how the information contributes to an understanding of the text in which it appears.

Name _____

Read the selection. Then answer the questions that follow.

An Old Game

You kick the ball down the field, and then pass it off to your friend who aims and | 18
kicks the ball towards the goal and scores! Your team wins another game, and all the | 34
while, you are thinking how some form of the game of soccer has been played for | 50
thousands of years. | 53

It's true—there's evidence that an exercise involving kicking a ball into a net was | 68
used by soldiers in China in about 100 to 200 BC. Another ball-kicking game was | 83
played in Japan even earlier than that. This game is still played today by children and | 99
adults. | 100

For a long time, people have been learning how to control a ball with their feet, | 116
and enjoying it. Today, soccer is the most popular game in the world, with millions of | 132
people playing and watching the sport. | 138

Soccer Timeline

| 1000 BC—In Japan, players kick ball around small field. Game is called "Kemari." | 100–200 BC—In China, soldiers train with ball-kicking game. Small leather ball is kicked into net held up by poles. Net's opening is only 11 to 15 inches wide! | AD 611—Japan and China play game against each other. | AD 700—In England, soccer-like game is played. Hundreds of people can play on one team! | AD 1600s—British colonists spread game around the world. | AD 1800s—In England, modern rules are set, and the size and weight of ball are made official. | AD 1960s—Television creates more awareness of game. It becomes more popular in U.S. |

Turn the page.

Answer the questions below.

1 The author most likely chose the title "An Old Game" because the selection is about

  A an activity meant for adults.

  (B) the history of soccer.

  C a soccer team from long ago.

  D how the sport died out.

2 What was probably the author's main reason for writing this selection?

  F to give an opinion about the game of soccer

  G to convince readers to join a soccer team

  H to teach readers how to pass the soccer ball

  (J) to share facts about the game of soccer

3 At the very beginning of the selection, why did the author describe someone playing soccer?

  A to show that the selection contains facts

  B to convince readers that soccer is a fun game

  (C) to interest readers in the topic of soccer

  D to describe the appearance of a soccer player

4 Readers can tell from the timeline that, before the 1800s, the balls used in soccer were

  (F) sometimes of different sizes.

  G weighed before each game.

  H larger than the balls used now.

  J always made out of leather.

5 Why did the author include information about soccer today?

  Possible response: In this history of soccer, the author wrote about today's soccer to show how the game has lasted over time and become prized by many people.

Common Core State Standards

Questions 1–3, 5: **Informational Text 8.** Explain how an author uses reasons and evidence to support particular points in a text. **Question 4: Informational Text 7.** Interpret information presented visually, orally, or quantitatively (e.g., in charts, graphs, diagrams, time lines, animations, or interactive elements on Web pages) and explain how the information contributes to an understanding of the text in which it appears.

Name _____

Read the selection. Then answer the questions that follow.

The White House

Home of the President

The White House has survived fire, war, and more than two hundred years of use. John Adams was the first President to reside there. In 1800, he and his wife moved into it before construction was finished and allowed work to continue around them.

Destroyed by Fire

During the war of 1812, British troops set the White House ablaze. Some people thought the building should be replaced, but President James Madison wanted it to remain unchanged. He wanted Americans to know their government was still strong. Since the outer walls were mostly still standing, the White House was rebuilt on the inside, with few changes made to the outside.

The West Wing

In 1901, President Theodore Roosevelt moved in with his wife and six children. At that time, the second floor held presidential offices in addition to living quarters for the first family. Roosevelt's large family needed more room, so a new western wing was constructed for the offices. The family could then occupy the whole second floor.

Much Needed Repairs

By the time Harry Truman became president in 1945, the White House was nearly 150 years old and desperately needed repairs. In fact, President Truman felt the entire inside needed rebuilding. He and his family moved into a building across the street. Bulldozers dug out a new basement, air conditioning and heating were installed, and fire protection was added. Four years later, a new White House stood inside those old, old walls.

4
19
36
48
51
65
78
90
105
113
116
130
145
159
172
175
190
204
218
232
247

The first design of the White House.

Turn the page.

Answer the questions below.

1 The White House shown in the drawing dates from *approximately*

(A) 1800.

B 1812.

C 1901.

D 1945.

2 Why did the author include paragraph headings in this selection?

F to show the reader when important events happened

(G) to let the reader know what each section is about

H to convince the reader that the author knows about the White House

J to encourage the reader to read more slowly

3 What is the most likely reason the author wrote this selection?

A to entertain readers with a sad story

B to express love for the United States

C to encourage readers to study history

(D) to present facts about the White House

4 In more than two hundred years much has happened at the White House. Why did the author choose to include only these four events?

These events show the major changes in the White House's 200-year history.

5 Why do you think the author organized information in chronological order?

Answers may vary. Possible responses: Telling events in the order they happened helps the reader keep history straight while reading. Any other order might be confusing.

Common Core State Standards

Question 1: Informational Text 7. Interpret information presented visually, orally, or quantitatively (e.g., in charts, graphs, diagrams, time lines, animations, or interactive elements on Web pages) and explain how the information contributes to an understanding of the text in which it appears. Questions 2–5: Informational Text 8. Explain how an author uses reasons and evidence to support particular points in a text.

Name _____

Read the selection. Then answer the questions that follow.

Grandma's Bookstore

Last Saturday, I helped Grandma in her bookstore. I wanted to play with my friends | 15

outside, but Grandma needed my assistance. Grandma's bookstore is tiny, dusty, and | 27

musty. It's not like a big, clean new store at the mall. Grandma calls it her old dinosaur. | 45

She only sells used books. | 50

Bored, I worked shelving a stack of children's books, most of which were for | 64

younger kids. Then one book about pirates, which was for boys like me, caught my | 79

attention. I paged through it, looking at the detailed, hand-painted pictures. Then I | 92

started to read. The story was really exciting! | 100

I finished my work and asked Grandma if I could keep the book. She said yes! | 116

Maybe the bookstore was not so bad after all, I thought. | 127

Turn the page.

Answer the questions below.

1   **To what does Grandma compare her store?**

    A   a library

    (B)   a dinosaur

    C   a market

    D   a playground

2   **How is Grandma's bookstore different from a new bookstore?**

    F   Grandma's store is in the mall.

    G   Grandma's store only sells children's books.

    (H)   Grandma's store is small and dusty.

    J   Grandma's store gives books away to strangers.

3   **Grandma wanted her grandson to come to the store because**

    (A)   she needed his help putting books away.

    B   she wanted to give him a book.

    C   she needed him to find books about pirates.

    D   she wanted to buy him a book.

4   **How does the boy change from the beginning to the end of the story?**

Possible response: At the beginning, the boy wants to play outside instead of be in the store. At the end, the boy does not mind the store so much because he finds a good book to read.

Common Core State Standards

Questions 1, 2: Literature 1. Refer to details and examples in a text when explaining what the text says explicitly and when drawing inferences from the text. Questions 3, 4: Literature 3. Describe in depth a character, setting, or event in a story or drama, drawing on specific details in a text (e.g., a character's thoughts, words, or actions).

Name _____

Read the selection. Then answer the questions that follow.

A Visit to an Old Friend

Last weekend, we went to stay with Mom's old roommate, Irene, who lives six | 14
hours away from us. Irene and Mom went to college together, but their lives have | 29
changed a lot since then. Mom moved to the city to live and work as a teacher—and | 47
marry my dad and have me—while Irene moved to a farm house way up near the | 64
border with Canada. Irene lives alone and works as a veterinarian taking care of farm | 79
animals, like pigs, yuck! | 83

When we drove up, the first thing I noticed was black smoke billowing out of | 98
Irene's roof. This was not a good sign. I knew I wouldn't like the country. | 113

"Hey, Mom," I cried. "I think the house is on fire!" Mom looked alarmed, and then | 129
she laughed. | 131

"That's the chimney, silly. It's for Irene's wood-burning stove. That's how she heats | 144
her house." | 146

How would I know? We lived in an apartment building with radiators. | 158

We carried our bags inside and greeted Irene, a tall, reed-thin woman with long | 172
braids. | 173

"You can help me split some logs, Gabe; we'll need more wood for tonight." Irene | 188
gestured to a small pile of wood next to the stove Mom had referred to earlier. | 204

Mom didn't let me attempt splitting logs, but I did help carry the wood inside. It | 220
was funny to be performing the tasks of a colonial settler. After that, we walked around | 236
and saw a stream, woods, and a big garden. I had to admit it was all beautiful. Country | 254
living would be acceptable, at least for a weekend! | 263

Turn the page.

Answer the questions below.

1 How is Irene's home different from Gabe's home?

(**A**) It has a wood stove.

B It is near the city.

C It has an apartment.

D It is heated.

2 According to the information given in the story, how are Mom and Irene alike?

F They both have one child.

G They both are teachers.

H They both have long hair.

(**J**) They both went to college.

3 To whom does Gabe compare himself in this story?

A a farmer

B a fire fighter

(**C**) a colonist

D a veterinarian

4 How did Gabe's feelings change from the beginning to the end of the story?

Possible response: In the beginning, he thought he didn't like the country. At the end, he liked it enough to spend a weekend there.

5 What happened in the story to make Gabe think differently?

Possible response: At the end, Gabe kind of enjoyed doing chores like carrying wood. He also liked the beautiful stream, woods, and garden. So he decided the country was not so bad.

> **Common Core State Standards**

Question 1: Literature 1. Refer to details and examples in a text when explaining what the text says explicitly and when drawing inferences from the text.
Questions 2–5: Literature 3. Describe in depth a character, setting, or event in a story or drama, drawing on specific details in a text (e.g., a character's thoughts, words, or actions).

- -

Name _____

Read the selection. Then answer the questions that follow.

The Wind Walker

Sarah's class had just finished reading a book called *The Wind Walker,* and the | 14

teacher asked students to create a picture of the book's main character. Sarah's twin | 28

sister, Gretchen, also had this assignment from her teacher. | 37

"His body is green and he has long, wavy hair," Gretchen announced, digging into | 51

the emerald paint with her brush. | 57

"I'm not sure what the wind walker looks like," Sarah commented. She rifled | 70

through the book's first few pages, hoping for an answer. | 80

Gretchen was busy, painting away. Sarah, however, still sat trying to conjure up the | 94

wind walker in her mind. | 99

"Just start painting, dear," Mom said to Sarah, "and it will come." | 111

"No, Mom. I want to plan it out first." | 120

Soon, Gretchen clipped her painting to a string that Dad had attached to the ceiling | 135

and ran outside to ride her bike, while Sarah still sat with a blank paper in front of her. | 154

She examined Gretchen's painting: That's not what the wind walker looks like, | 166

she mused. His hair is not that long, and his body is blue, not green. Gretchen's figure | 183

looks like a green giant. The wind walker has a serene smile on his face, not that awful | 201

smirk Gretchen gave him, and he walks on the air, not the mountaintops. | 214

Suddenly, Sarah feverishly started in on her work, and in a few minutes, she was | 229

finished. Sarah thought her picture was more accurate than Gretchen's, but Mom would | 242

probably say they were just different. | 248

Turn the page.

Answer the questions below.

1 From the story, what was one difference between Sarah's and Gretchen's pictures?

    A the materials

    B the paper

    C the colors

    D the subject

2 To which of these did Sarah compare Gretchen's wind walker?

    F a backpacker

    G a visitor

    H a mountaintop

    J a giant

3 What was the same about Sarah's and Gretchen's wind walkers in this story?

    A They were both green.

    B They were both men.

    C They were both evil.

    D They were both laughing.

4 What is one way that Sarah and her sister Gretchen were different? Support your answer with details from the story.

Possible responses: Gretchen worked quickly, and Sarah took her time. Gretchen finished her painting fast, and Sarah finished hers later, after more thought.

5 What happened that helped Sarah figure out what she wanted to paint?

She looked at Gretchen's painting and discovered the ways it was different from her own ideas about the wind walker.

Common Core State Standards

Questions 1–3: Literature 1. Refer to details and examples in a text when explaining what the text says explicitly and when drawing inferences from the text. Questions 4, 5: Literature 3. Describe in depth a character, setting, or event in a story or drama, drawing on specific details in a text (e.g., a character's thoughts, words, or actions).

Read the selection. Then answer the questions that follow.

Bringing Rana Home

As soon as the Silvas returned from their vacation, Alonso pleaded with his mother	14
to pick up Rana, the family's Labrador retriever. The dog had stayed with another	28
family while the Silvas were on vacation, and Alonso could hardly wait to see her. Mrs.	44
Silva telephoned their friends and asked if they could pick up Rana.	56
When the door opened, Rana rushed out and threw herself at Alonso. He and his	71
mother laughed and thanked their friends for caring for the dog.	82
At first, Rana rode in the front seat of the car, her head hanging out of the window.	100
She barked at everyone they passed, as if to exclaim, "My family has returned, after all!	116
Isn't it wonderful?"	119
Mrs. Silva soon grew tired of Rana's barking and rolled up the window, despite	133
whimpers from the dog. Alonso slapped his hands on his thighs and said, "Come sit in	149
back with me, Rana." She went to him, her brown eyes full of gladness.	163

Turn the page.

Answer the questions below.

1 **What is the theme of this story?**

(A) Children and pet dogs like to be together.

B Dogs should not be allowed to ride in cars.

C Vacations without dogs are not any fun.

D Children should take their dogs on walks.

2 **Which of the following *best* describes Rana in this story?**

F poorly trained by the Silvas

(G) happy to be back with Alonso

H upset about riding in the car

J scared to stay with new people

3 **What is Alonso's problem at the *beginning* of the story?**

A His mother missed Rana.

B Alonso thanked the Silvas' friends.

C Rana barked out the window.

(D) Alonso missed Rana.

4 **Why do you think the author *most likely* wrote this selection?**

Answers may vary. Possible response: The author probably wanted to tell an entertaining story about how a boy and his dog had missed each other and were happy to be back together again.

Common Core State Standards

Question 1: Literature 2. Determine a theme of a story, drama, or poem from details in the text; summarize the text. **Questions 2, 3: Literature 3.** Describe in depth a character, setting, or event in a story or drama, drawing on specific details in a text (e.g., a character's thoughts, words, or actions). **Question 4: Literature 1.** Refer to details and examples in a text when explaining what the text says explicitly and when drawing inferences from the text.

Fresh Reads   Unit 5 Week 3 SI

Name _____

Read the selection. Then answer the questions that follow.

The Race

The children lined up in the middle of the dirt road. Jesse, the oldest, stood on the | 17
far side, leaning forward. Beside him, Thomas stuffed a paperback book into the pocket | 31
of his pants. Next came Mary, tall and relaxed, only an inch or two shorter than Jesse. | 48
Ruthie was on the end. She studied the row of bare feet in the dust. They were all | 66
bigger than hers, all fidgety and itching to run. | 75

Ruthie counted, "One, two, three, go!" A spatter of gravel and dust flew out behind | 90
Jesse as he took off running, leaving the others behind. Mary's muscular legs carried | 104
her away too, and even Thomas showed Ruthie his back. She didn't mind. She was glad | 120
to be racing with her older cousins—there was never any thought that she would win. | 136

Thomas soon slowed to a walk, holding his side with one hand. Ruthie caught | 150
up and walked with him. Jesse reached the pine tree at the bend in the road, touched | 167
its trunk, and started back. Seconds later, Mary did the same. They sprinted toward | 181
Thomas and Ruthie, who stopped to watch. | 188

Ruthie remembered that Mary had insisted the race must be to the tree and back. | 203
"That's a long way to run," Jesse had said. | 212

Mary had replied, "Maybe you can run faster, but I can run farther." | 225

Jesse had laughed, not really believing her. | 232

As Ruthie and Thomas watched, Mary proved it. Barely ahead of Mary, Jesse | 245
struggled up to the younger cousins. In that moment, Mary lowered her chin and | 259
smiled. Her feet pounded the dusty road, making a soft sound: *slap, slap, slap, slap.* | 274
She ran by with a wink for Ruthie and passed Jesse without even breathing hard. | 289

Turn the page.

Answer the questions below.

1 **What is the theme of this story?**

A You should try to run races slowly and carefully.

B Running races can mean both time and distance.

C It is better to be able to race fast than to run far.

D Younger children can race as fast as older ones.

2 **What happened *after* Ruthie yelled, "One, two, three, go!"?**

F Jesse took off, leaving the others behind.

G Mary took the lead, leaving Jesse behind.

H Thomas and Ruthie walked together.

J Ruthie stood at the end of the line of cousins.

3 **Which of these *best* describes Jesse as a runner in this story?**

A slow and tired too soon

B slow but able to run far

C fast but tired too soon

D fast and able to run far

4 **What was *probably* the main reason the author wrote this selection?**

F To entertain readers with a story

G To explain how to win a foot race

H To teach readers to be good losers

J To describe some family members

5 **Why did Mary smile at Ruthie and Thomas just before she passed Jesse?**

Mary had confidence in herself, and she liked to win.

_____

_____

_____

_____

Common Core State Standards

Question 1: Literature 2. Determine a theme of a story, drama, or poem from details in the text; summarize the text. **Questions 2, 4: Literature 1.** Refer to details and examples in a text when explaining what the text says explicitly and when drawing inferences from the text. **Questions 3, 5: Literature 3.** Describe in depth a character, setting, or event in a story or drama, drawing on specific details in a text (e.g., a character's thoughts, words, or actions).

Name _____

Read the selection. Then answer the questions that follow.

A Little More Carefully

Kevin had never gone to Canada until he visited his Uncle Paul. He knew some	15
things would be unfamiliar. For example, Canadian television shows were unique. He	27
also knew that his uncle spoke both French and English. Soon, Kevin realized another	41
significant difference.	43
Uncle Paul offered Kevin an unexpected gift in a tiny white box that jingled when	58
Kevin accepted it. "Can you guess what's in there?" Uncle Paul asked.	70
"Coins," Kevin guessed, grinning.	74
"*Oui*," said Uncle Paul, "and I hope it's enough to purchase a new baseball cap."	89
Uncle Paul knew that Kevin collected baseball caps of all colors and logos. When	103
Kevin opened the box and saw five quarters, he felt disappointed.	114
Kevin did not have the heart to tell his uncle that the average baseball cap cost a lot	132
more than five quarters. "*Merci*, Uncle Paul. I'll save these quarters to buy a new hat."	148
Uncle Paul chuckled at his naive nephew. "You think those are quarters, but each	162
of those coins is worth $2. That's how we do it here in Montreal." He gave Kevin an	180
affectionate slap on the back.	185
A little embarrassed, Kevin picked up one of the coins, held it up in the sunlight,	201
and recognized that it didn't look like a quarter at all. Now that he was in a different	219
country, it was clear that he should look at everything a little more carefully.	233
"Come on, we can still catch the downtown bus if we hurry," said Uncle Paul, "and	249
I guarantee we'll find just the right cap."	257

Turn the page.

Answer the questions below.

1 Why were the coins important to this story?

   A They bought Kevin a new baseball cap.

   (B) They were worth more than Kevin thought.

   C They were quarters.

   D They came in a white box.

2 What is *probably* the main reason the author wrote this selection?

   F to teach readers about Canadian money

   G to explain to tourists what Canada is like

   H to tell how much a baseball cap can cost

   (J) to entertain readers with an amusing story

3 Why did Uncle Paul chuckle in the middle of the story?

   (A) He knew that Kevin had gotten the wrong idea.

   B He thought Kevin spoke French in a funny way.

   C He was very happy to see his favorite nephew.

   D He thought that collecting baseball caps was silly.

4 What is the theme of this story?

Possible response: Things in a new place may be different from the way they are at home.

5 What made Kevin feel disappointed in the middle of the story?

Kevin feels disappointed because he thinks the five coins are quarters, which would not be enough money to buy a new baseball cap.

Common Core State Standards

Questions 1, 2: Literature 1. Refer to details and examples in a text when explaining what the text says explicitly and when drawing inferences from the text. Questions 3, 5: Literature 3. Describe in depth a character, setting, or event in a story or drama, drawing on specific details in a text (e.g., a character's thoughts, words, or actions). Question 4: Literature 2. Determine a theme of a story, drama, or poem from details in the text; summarize the text.

Read the selection. Then answer the questions that follow.

Science Class Studies Litter Problem

Roadsides around here are much cleaner this week than last. We can thank	13
fourth-grade students at Wells Creek School and their science teacher, Diana Paz.	25
These students spent most of last Saturday and Sunday collecting roadside trash.	37
The cleanup is part of a project the class is working on. These students want to	53
know how much litter drivers in this area throw out on the road each month. Students	69
will work one weekend out of every month until the end of the school year. They will	86
gather trash in plastic bags and weigh it. Last weekend, students collected more than	101
one hundred pounds of trash!	105
Ten parents helped the hardworking students. Some of those parents will not be	118
able to help next month. More volunteers will be needed. If you are able to take part,	135
call Wells Creek School and ask for Ms. Paz.	144

Turn the page.

Answer the questions below.

1 **What is the main idea of the last paragraph?**

A Ten parents helped the hardworking students.

B Some of those parents will not be able to help next month.

(C) More volunteers will be needed.

D If you are able to take part, call Wells Creek School and ask for Ms. Paz.

2 **What conclusion can readers draw about Ms. Paz and her students?**

(F) They believed litter was an important problem.

G They often threw litter on the ground.

H They worked hard every weekend.

J They took part in many science projects.

3 **When did the students collect roadside trash?**

A every day before school

B during science class

C every weekend

(D) one weekend every month

4 **Write the main idea of the selection and at least one detail that supports it.**

The main idea is that students picked up roadside trash as part of a science project. Supporting details may vary. For example: Students picked up more than one hundred pounds.

Common Core State Standards

Questions 1, 4: Informational Text 2. Determine the main idea of a text and explain how it is supported by key details; summarize the text.
Questions 2, 3: Informational Text 1. Refer to details and examples in a text when explaining what the text says explicitly and when drawing inferences from the text.

Name _____

Read the selection. Then answer the questions that follow.

Catch a Wave

You feel the sun's warmth on your back. The surfboard under your belly is warm	15
too. You paddle out toward deeper water. Saltwater splashes in your eyes. You hear the	30
ocean's roar. You reach a place where whitecaps form on the tops of waves. You paddle	46
farther. Finally, you are there, outside of the breaking waves.	56

The Ride

58
It's time to catch a wave. One comes toward you, and it's big. You paddle ahead of	75
it back toward shore. The wave lifts your board high in the air. You stand up on your	93
board. You use your feet to balance. You move back a little and use your arms. That's	110
better. This is what it means to catch a wave.	120
You're flying across the face of a wave that is huge—taller than you. Your surfboard	136
slices into the water like a great knife. You taste salt in your mouth, and something else	153
too. You taste excitement!	157

The Board

159
Things have changed since the first British explorers reported seeing Hawaiians	170
surfing. Those Hawaiians used wooden boards. Most of today's surfboards are made of	183
plastic foam covered with a hard shell. Many surfers use "shortboards" because they	196
are fast and easier to maneuver. Other surfers prefer "longboards," which are more than	210
seven feet long.	213
For that matter, you don't have to use a board to surf. Many surfers ride the waves	230
without boards—it's called *bodysurfing*. It isn't the board that matters most. It's the	244
ride.	245

Turn the page.

Answer the questions below.

1 What sentence from the selection tells the main idea of the section subtitled "The Ride"?

(A) It's time to catch a wave.

B One comes toward you, and it's big.

C You stand up on your board.

D You use your feet to balance.

2 According to the selection, what does a surfer do when a big wave is coming?

F sits very still

G stands up quickly

H swims past it

(J) paddles ahead of it

3 What is the selection mostly about?

A british explorers

B hawaii

(C) surfing

D ocean swimming

4 How would you verify the truth of the statements of fact in the final section of the selection?

Answers may vary. Possible response: I would look up "surfing history" or "surf boards" on the Internet.

5 How does the title support the main idea of the selection?

The main idea of the selection is that surfing is fun and exciting. Catching a wave is the start of that adventure.

Common Core State Standards

Questions 1, 3, 5: Informational Text 2. Determine the main idea of a text and explain how it is supported by key details; summarize the text.
Questions 2, 4: Informational Text 1. Refer to details and examples in a text when explaining what the text says explicitly and when drawing inferences from the text.

Read the selection. Then answer the questions that follow.

Feeling Bad?

Everyone experiences it sometime. Your legs feel weak, you are tired, and you have	14
no energy. Perhaps your head hurts. You feel cold, and no matter what you do, you	30
can't warm up. However, the school nurse feels your forehead, says it's hot, and then	45
checks your temperature. It is one hundred and two. You have a fever.	58
Fever is an increase in body temperature. For most people, normal body	70
temperature is between ninety-eight and ninety-nine degrees Fahrenheit. It can rise if a	83
person sits for a while in a very hot place, such as a sauna. If it does, the brain tells the	104
body to sweat. The person feels the need to go someplace cool. These responses help	119
the body cool itself. Body temperature can also rise when a person is sick.	133
Fever is not a sickness. It is how the body responds to sickness or sometimes an	149
injury. When a virus enters the body, the brain knows it is there. It tries to fight it off.	168
Experts believe that fever speeds up the body's reaction to the virus. The same thing	183
can happen because of an allergy, bacterial infection, or poison.	193
Fever can be dangerous if it rises too high, so we usually try to get rid of it. One	212
way to do this is to relax in a cool bath. Certain kinds of medicine are also sometimes	230
helpful. A nurse or doctor can help you and your family know the best way to handle a	248
fever.	249

Turn the page.

Answer the questions below.

1 What sentence in the second paragraph states the paragraph's main idea?

(A) Fever is an increase in body temperature.

B It can rise if a person sits for a while in a very hot place, such as a sauna.

C The person feels the need to go someplace cool.

D Body temperature can also rise when a person is sick.

2 According to the selection, what is one reason fever happens?

F sweating

(G) illness

H lost energy

J cold weather

3 What is the selection about?

A virus

B doctors

(C) fever

D medicine

4 How would you verify that normal body temperature is ninety-eight to ninety-nine degrees Fahrenheit?

Answers may vary. Possible response: I would look up this information in a medical book or a book about the human body.

5 Write the main idea of the last paragraph, and give at least one detail that supports it.

We usually want to get rid of a fever. You can take medicine or a cool bath, or get advice from a doctor.

Common Core State Standards

Questions 1, 3, 5: Informational Text 2. Determine the main idea of a text and explain how it is supported by key details; summarize the text.
Questions 2, 4: Informational Text 1. Refer to details and examples in a text when explaining what the text says explicitly and when drawing inferences from the text.

Name _____

Read the selection. Then answer the questions that follow.

Mrs. Woodruff's Tortoise

A tortoise lived in Mrs. Woodruff's garden. It was fond of vegetables, and Mrs.	14
Woodruff was happy to let it have some. After all, it ate very little.	28
One day, Mrs. Woodruff came out and discovered the tortoise sadly observing a row	42
of lettuce nubs. The entire row of lettuce had been eaten. She angrily scooped up the	58
tortoise to banish it from her garden. "How could you steal my lettuce after I trusted	74
you to take only what you needed?"	81
The tortoise just ducked its head into its shell.	90
Mrs. Woodruff heard her own words, though. She realized that she really had	103
trusted the tortoise because it had never taken more than a little bit. Some other creature	119
must have been in her garden. She gently set down the tortoise inside the garden fence,	135
glad that she had thought things through.	142

Turn the page.

Answer the questions below.

1 Why did Mrs. Woodruff let the tortoise live in her garden?

A She thought that tortoises did not eat plants.

B It only ate weeds and other plants she did not want.

C She knew it would never eat much.

D She wanted it to chase away other animals.

2 What did Mrs. Woodruff think when she first saw that the lettuce had been eaten?

F The tortoise had eaten the lettuce.

G The lettuce wasn't growing very fast.

H The lettuce had died.

J She had picked it herself and forgotten.

3 What is the story's theme?

A Never trust anyone.

B Always think before you act.

C Be kind to animals.

D Don't take more than you need.

4 Do you think it was a good idea to put the tortoise back in the garden?

Answers may vary. Possible responses: It wasn't a good idea because if something got into the garden again, Mrs. Woodruff would probably think it was the tortoise. It was a good idea because Mrs. Woodruff remembered that the tortoise doesn't eat very much.

> **Common Core State Standards**

Questions 1, 2, 4: **Literature 1.** Refer to details and examples in a text when explaining what the text says explicitly and when drawing inferences from the text. **Question 3: Literature 2.** Determine a theme of a story, drama, or poem from details in the text; summarize the text.

Name _____

Read the selection. Then answer the questions that follow.

The House

When Carrie's family moved into the Samuels' old house, it was in pretty bad | 14

shape. Inside the house, wallpaper sagged off the wall in wide strips. The kitchen stove | 29

did not work, and the window was broken. The front steps were downright scary. So | 44

many boards were missing that she could see the ground underneath. Carrie said to her | 59

mother, "Do we have to live in this house? It's a disaster." | 71

Carrie's mother only smiled and said, "We can put it together. All it needs is a | 87

little TLC." | 89

Carrie knew that TLC stood for "tender, loving care." What she didn't understand | 102

was why her mother couldn't see that the house needed more than that. It needed a | 118

wrecking ball. | 120

Still, she helped her mom repair the broken window in the kitchen. When a truck | 135

rolled up with a new stove, Carrie helped move the old one out of the way. She helped | 153

her mother pull off the peeling wallpaper. Then, she helped paint the living room walls | 168

a bright, happy yellow. Fixing the steps was a big job. Carrie's mother borrowed an | 183

electric saw from a friend. Then, she borrowed the friend to help her use it. Carrie | 199

helped too, measuring and holding boards in place while the friend hammered and | 212

sawed. | 213

When the steps were repaired, Carrie ran up and down, laughing. "Look at this!" | 227

she shouted. "This house is not so bad after all." | 237

Her mother only smiled and said, "All it needed was a little TLC." | 250

Turn the page.

Answer the questions below.

1 The words Carrie uses to describe the house suggest that

   A a new kitchen was needed.

   B a few repairs were needed.

   C it needed cleaning.

   (D) it needed to be torn down.

2 How did Carrie feel about moving into the house?

   (F) unhappy

   G excited

   H proud

   J embarrassed

3 Which of the following best describes Carrie's mother?

   A bossy

   B lazy

   (C) hardworking

   D softhearted

4 What did Carrie learn in the story?

   F Everything looks better when it's painted yellow.

   (G) A lot can be done if you're willing to work hard.

   H Family is the most important thing.

   J You should always measure carefully.

5 How did Carrie feel after the steps were fixed? Give details from the story to support your answer.

She was excited and hopeful. We know because she ran up and down the steps laughing, and she said the house might turn out OK after all.

Common Core State Standards

Question 1: Literature 1. Refer to details and examples in a text when explaining what the text says explicitly and when drawing inferences from the text.
Questions 2–5: Literature 3. Describe in depth a character, setting, or event in a story or drama, drawing on specific details in a text (e.g., a character's thoughts, words, or actions).

Name _____

Read the selection. Then answer the questions that follow.

The Apple Does Not Roll Far

Wai Ling's great-grandfather had been a famous maker of clay pottery. His	13
name was mentioned in many books, and his clay pots and bowls could be found in	28
museums.	29
The family possessed only one of the great-grandfather's bowls. It rested on a	42
high shelf, a king of bowls. Wai Ling often stared at it, admiring the strong shape and	59
delicate colors, and wished that she could make something just as lovely.	71
Her parents knew of her wish and gave her a box of clay. She tried to mold it into a	91
bowl with a strong shape, like her great-grandfather's bowl. When it was finished, she	105
didn't like looking at it. Making bowls was harder than she had thought.	118
Her father saw it and said, "The apple does not roll far from the tree."	133
He meant that she was like her great-grandfather, a maker of fine clay pottery. Wai	148
Ling rolled her eyes, certain that he only liked it because he was her father. She stepped	165
in front of the bowl so he could not see it.	176
Her father took down the great-grandfather's bowl, and Wai Ling touched it,	188
gingerly. The clay was grainy and the color was hard to name because it changed in the	205
light. Sometimes it was a deep reddish-brown, sometimes green like moss growing next	218
to a river.	221
Her father said, "He made this bowl when he was eighty-seven. He had spent his	236
whole life learning to make it. Do you think his first bowl was like this?"	251
Wai Ling shook her head. She knew that a person did not learn to make something	267
so special in one afternoon—it would take a lifetime.	277

Turn the page.

- -

Answer the questions below.

1 What did Wai Ling expect would happen when her parents gave her the clay?

   A She expected to spend her life learning how to make bowls.

   B She thought her parents would show her how to use it.

   C She was afraid to try to make anything with it.

   (D) She thought she would make a beautiful bowl.

2 What did Wai Ling's father mean when he said, "The apple does not roll far from the tree"?

   F He wanted to put the bowl on the shelf.

   G He wanted to put apples in the bowl.

   (H) He thought she had her great-grandfather's talent.

   J He thought she should begin by making fruit.

3 How did Wai Ling feel about her bowl at first?

   A She liked the colors.

   (B) She felt disappointed.

   C She wanted to show it to her father at once.

   D She thought it was too much like her great-grandfather's bowl.

4 What did Wai Ling learn by touching and looking closely at the old bowl?

Answers may vary. Possible response: She learned to appreciate how beautiful and well made it was.

5 What is the theme of the story? Give at least one detail from the story to support your answer.

Learning takes time—no one is an expert the first time he or she tries something. Wai Ling learned this in the last paragraph, when she realized that her great-grandfather had spent his life learning how to make bowls.

Common Core State Standards

Questions 1–4: Literature 3. Describe in depth a character, setting, or event in a story or drama, drawing on specific details in a text (e.g., a character's thoughts, words, or actions). Question 5: Literature 2. Determine a theme of a story, drama, or poem from details in the text; summarize the text.

Read the selection. Then answer the questions that follow.

Beetles

There are an awful lot of beetles on this Earth. In fact, there are more than 300,000	17
different kinds—that we know about.	23
Ladybugs are one kind of beetle that people enjoy having around. Gardeners like	36
them because they eat plant-eating insects. Some people even buy boxes of ladybugs to	50
set free in their gardens.	55
Not all beetles are good neighbors, though. The boll weevil beetle destroys cotton	68
crops in many parts of the world. Then there is the Japanese beetle—it eats the leaves	85
of plants, causing the plants to die.	92
In certain tropical areas, beetles grow to be larger than your hand. They have wide,	107
fanlike antennae. Their wings glitter in wonderful shades of blue and green. They are	121
prized by people who collect beetles. That's right—some people collect beetles, and	134
they pay hundreds of dollars for very special ones.	143

Turn the page.

Answer the questions below.

1 Why do some people release ladybugs in their gardens?

A They are the most beautiful bugs.

B Their bright color frightens away beetles.

(C) They eat harmful insects.

D They bring fireflies to the gardens.

2 What happens when Japanese beetles attack plants?

F The beetles grow larger than your hand.

G The beetles become good neighbors.

H The plants turn yellow but are still healthy.

(J) The beetles eat the leaves, killing the plants.

3 Which sentence from the selection *best* states the main idea?

A Not all beetles are good neighbors, though.

B In certain tropical areas, beetles grow to be larger than your hand.

(C) There are a lot of beetles on this Earth.

D Ladybugs are one kind of beetle that people enjoy having around.

4 What do you think would happen if everyone started collecting beetles?

Answers may vary. Possible response: Beetles would probably disappear pretty quickly, especially the colorful ones that are prized by collectors. Then, maybe laws would be passed against collecting beetles. Or perhaps some people may start beetle farms.

Common Core State Standards

Questions 1, 2, 4: Informational Text 3. Explain events, procedures, ideas, or concepts in a historical, scientific, or technical text, including what happened and why, based on specific information in the text. Question 3: Informational Text 2. Determine the main idea of a text and explain how it is supported by key details; summarize the text.

Name _____

Read the selection. Then answer the questions that follow.

Water Expert Comes to Sage City!

Clear, cold water tumbling down a mountain stream is a beautiful sound. On a	14
hot summer day, when throats are scratchy and dry, water tastes better than anything.	28
When rain has not fallen for two months, when our skin is cracking and grass is turning	45
brown, raindrops on our face feel better than anything in the world. Water is important	60
stuff.	61
Author Wyatt Cameron wants people to think about that, and he's coming to Sage	75
City to tell us how. His latest book, *Don't Waste Our Water,* is about using water wisely.	92
Many of his ideas are simple: Set out barrels in your garden to catch rainwater, and	108
then use it to water your crops. If you must have a lawn, you should plant grass that	126
grows naturally in your area. It will need less water to survive. To wash your car, pour	143
water in a bucket instead of letting the hose run over the car. *Don't Waste Our Water*	160
also has ideas for farmers, ranchers, and city governments.	169
As most readers know, the Sage City area has had very little rainfall over the past	185
three years. Piney Creek, which supplies many ranches and farms, carries about half	198
as much water as it did five years ago. Wells are drying up. Crops are dying. Ranchers	215
have had to sell off cattle. It's time to make some changes.	227
If you want to know more about saving water, come to Sage City Hall this Saturday	243
at noon. Wyatt Cameron will be there to sign books and teach us all a thing or two	261
about saving water. Come on out and listen. You'll be glad you did!	274

Fresh Reads   Unit 6 Week 1 OL

153

Copyright © Pearson Education, Inc., or its affiliates. All Rights Reserved.

Answer the questions below.

1 According to the selection, if people put water in a bucket to wash cars
- **(A)** they will use less water.
- **B** it will be less messy.
- **C** they will get the car cleaner.
- **D** it will take less time.

2 What happened to cause wells to dry up?
- **F** Farmers and ranchers used too much water.
- **G** The wells were dug in the wrong places.
- **H** People in town used too much water.
- **(J)** There hadn't been enough rain.

3 Which sentence from the selection *best* states the main idea?
- **A** *Don't Waste Our Water* also has ideas for farmers, ranchers, and city governments.
- **B** If you must have a lawn, you should plant grass that grows naturally in your area.
- **(C)** Wyatt Cameron will be there to sign books and teach us all a thing or two about saving water.
- **D** Clear, cold water tumbling down a mountain stream is a beautiful sound.

4 What makes saving water especially important to farmers and ranchers?
- **F** It rains less often on farms and ranches.
- **(G)** They need water to make crops grow and for animals to drink.
- **H** They count on water from rivers, and these sometimes dry up.
- **J** It is hot on farms and ranches, so people get thirsty.

5 Think of ways to save water that are not listed in the selection. Describe at least one thing you can do that will save water.

Answers may vary. Possible response: I can turn the water off when I'm brushing my teeth, and I can tell a janitor when the faucet won't turn off in the school restroom.

4 Copyright © Pearson Education, Inc., or its affiliates. All Rights Reserved.

Common Core State Standards

Questions 1, 2, 4, 5: Informational Text 3. Explain events, procedures, ideas, or concepts in a historical, scientific, or technical text, including what happened and why, based on specific information in the text. **Question 3: Informational Text 2.** Determine the main idea of a text and explain how it is supported by key details; summarize the text.

Name _____

Read the selection. Then answer the questions that follow.

Mysterious Moon

On a clear, moonlit night, we can see the face of the "Man in the Moon." Even	17
without a telescope, we see shadows and shapes, bright and dark areas. Of course, there	32
is not really a man up there, but if we use our imaginations, it isn't hard to find the	51
outline of a face.	55
For thousands of years, people wondered about those shadows and shapes. Now we	68
no longer wonder, for people have visited the moon—taken photos, collected rocks and	82
dust. Cameras and robots have explored the moon, answering questions that puzzled	94
astronomers for centuries.	97
The light areas on the moon are called *terrae* (TEHR ee), which means "lands" in	112
Latin. We now know that these areas are mountainous. Some of the moon's mountain	126
ranges are as high as the Earth's Himalayas.	134
Long ago, the darker parts of the moon were thought to be oceans. They were	149
named *maria* (MAHR ee ah), derived from the Latin word for "oceans." We have since	164
learned that these areas are covered with dark rock. Ages ago, volcanoes poured lava	178
over the moon's surface. The lava cooled and became hard, leaving dark, smooth rock.	192
Seen from Earth, it looks a bit like water.	201
Both light and dark areas are dotted with craters. Most of these were formed when	216
meteors and other objects struck the moon, a long time ago. Once in a while, meteors	232
still strike the moon, and they still form craters. Incredibly, astronomers have seen it	246
happen.	247
Don't feel sad if, the next time you look up at the moon, you see mountains	263
and rock instead of a man's face. Think of the amazing science that brought us our	279
knowledge. Think of the "Man on the Moon"—Neil Armstrong—who walked on its	293
surface in 1969.	296

Turn the page.

Answer the questions below.

1 What happened on the moon to create dark areas?

    A Mountains rose up, casting shadows on some parts.

    (B) Volcanoes erupted and poured out lava.

    C People visited the moon, bringing dark dust from the Earth.

    D Comets struck the moon and started fires.

2 What caused the craters on the Moon's surface?

    F Ancient oceans dried up.

    (G) Meteors collided with the moon.

    H Volcanoes exploded and left great holes.

    J Earthquakes opened up cracks in the moon.

3 What is this selection mainly about?

    A the man in the moon

    B the moon's craters

    C the meteors on the moon

    (D) the moon's surface

4 Why are the dark areas on the moon called *maria?*

People once thought they were oceans, and *maria* means "oceans" in Latin.

5 Why might you no longer see a man's face when you look at the moon?

Possible answers: We now know the light and dark areas are mountains and craters; I imagine Neil Armstrong walking on the moon instead.

Common Core State Standards

Questions 1, 2, 4, 5: Informational Text 3. Explain events, procedures, ideas, or concepts in a historical, scientific, or technical text, including what happened and why, based on specific information in the text. **Question 3: Informational Text 2.** Determine the main idea of a text and explain how it is supported by key details; summarize the text.

Name _____

Read the selection. Then answer the questions that follow.

Zoo Trip

My little cousin, Sam, was excited because my mom and I were taking him on his | 16
first trip to the zoo. We started early Saturday on a beautiful two-hour drive along the | 32
ocean. | 33

Our first stop was the reptile house where we saw snakes, lizards, crocodiles, | 46
alligators, and turtles. The alligators frightened Sam because of their enormous jaws | 58
and sharp teeth. | 61

The next stop was the aquarium, with huge tanks and only a long glass window | 76
between us and the fish. Sam jumped because the big shark with its huge mouth | 91
seemed so close when it swam to the window. | 100

After a good lunch we visited the wild cat park. The tiger, the largest member of | 116
the cat family, looked huge, powerful, and fierce. Three tiger cubs that were sleeping | 130
looked soft and warm and reminded Sam of his own kitten. Mom laughed, "Remember, | 144
Sam, they grow up to be big tigers." | 152

Sam smiled. "I'm glad my cat won't get that big." | 162

Turn the page.

Answer the questions below.

1 Which of the following is a statement of fact?

   A My little cousin, Sam, was excited.

   (**B**) My mom and I were taking him on his first trip to the zoo.

   C We started early Saturday on a beautiful two-hour drive.

   D The tiger looked huge, powerful, and fierce.

2 Which sentence is a statement of opinion?

   (**F**) Alligators are the most frightening kind of animal.

   G The next stop was the aquarium.

   H The tiger is the largest member of the cat family.

   J Three tiger cubs reminded Sam of his own kitten.

3 What conclusion can you draw from the following sentence?

   "Sam jumped because the big shark with its huge mouth seemed so close when it swam to the window."

   A The shark was hungry and hunting.

   B The shark followed and attacked Sam.

   C The shark was excited and laughing.

   (**D**) The shark surprised and scared Sam.

4 Write one statement of opinion from the story about the tiger cubs.

Possible answer: The tiger cubs looked soft and warm.

_____

_____

_____

_____

_____

_____

Common Core State Standards

Questions 1–4: Literature 1. Refer to details and examples in a text when explaining what the text says explicitly and when drawing inferences from the text.

158

Fresh Reads   Unit 6 Week 2 SI

Name _____

Read the selection. Then answer the questions that follow.

Bird Watching

My best friend, Carlos, and I wanted to go bird watching. We went to the Nature	16
Center at the nearby forest reserve, where we picked up a trail map and a book with	33
many drawings and photographs of various birds in the area. The park ranger talked to	48
us about hiking in the woods and told us about birds we might see.	62
"You boys have fun. Follow the trail and keep your eyes open."	74
We gathered the necessary items: a forest service map, two bottles of water, snacks,	88
a compass for direction, and a whistle for emergencies.	97
Two weeks ago, on a beautiful, sunny day, we set out for our destination, Brown	112
Lake, which was two miles away. I led the way up a narrow trail through a thick forest.	130
We turned north, crossed a creek, climbed a steep hill, and headed east along a high	146
ridge. I spotted some beautiful little birds flying among the low bushes.	158
Suddenly I heard the sharp sound of a whistle. I quickly turned back, fearful of	173
what I might find, and ran toward Carlos, who was kneeling next to a wounded bird	189
that was lying on the ground. It was breathing hard, and its wing appeared to be broken.	206
Carlos was almost in tears, and I was shaking with fright, but we kept our cool and	223
did not panic. I carefully picked up the bird, wrapping it in my sweater, and held it	240
gently as we hurried back to the Center. We were relieved that the bird was still alive.	257
Yesterday we heard from the ranger that the bird had recovered and was ready to be	273
released. We went to the Center and showed our map to the ranger, pointing out where	289
we had found the bird. We had no doubt the bird would find its way home.	305

Turn the page.

Answer the questions below.

1 Which of the following is a statement of opinion?

  A We gathered the necessary items.

  B Two weeks ago, we set out for our destination.

  C I ran back toward Carlos.

  (D) I spotted some beautiful little birds.

2 The author writes, "I spotted some beautiful little birds flying among the low bushes." Which of the following best describes that statement?

  F It is a statement of fact.

  G It is a statement of opinion.

  (H) It is a statement of fact and opinion.

  J It is not a true statement.

3 The author writes, "We had no doubt the bird would find its way home." Which of the following best describes that statement?

  A It is a statement of fact.

  (B) It is a statement of opinion.

  C It is a statement of fact and opinion.

  D It is not a true statement.

4 What conclusion can you draw from the last paragraph of this selection?

  (F) The park ranger helped the bird get well.

  G The bird had flown among the low bushes.

  H The boys should have left the bird alone.

  J The bird watchers had photographed the bird.

5 Write one statement of fact about Carlos.

Answers may vary. Possible response: He found a wounded
bird on the trail.

Common Core State Standards

Questions 1–5: Literature 1. Refer to details and examples in a text when explaining what the text says explicitly and when drawing inferences from the text.

Name _____

Read the selection. Then answer the questions that follow.

Snowball

In 2003, the zoo in my city bought a male white tiger. His name is Snowball, and   17
he was born in a wildlife park somewhere in the United States. His ancestors were from   33
forests in central India. At the age of seven months, he traveled by airplane to our zoo.   50
Now he is two years old and will probably live another twenty years.   63

There are very few white tigers in the world. These rare, beautiful creatures have   77
sparkling blue eyes, rosy-pink noses, and buttery white fur with brown stripes from   90
head to tail. They are as tall as a fourth grader, twice as long, and five times heavier,   108
with a tail that measures three to four feet. They are good swimmers but poor climbers,   124
slow runners but stealthy and accomplished hunters. When hungry or sick, they have   137
been known to attack and kill people.   144

Over the years, hunters have killed and sold these animals for large amounts of   158
money. Population growth has destroyed much of the forests and grasslands where they   171
live, and today no known white tigers remain in the wild. These animals can now be   187
seen only in zoos or wildlife parks.   194

Tigers are solitary animals. Snowball seems happy in his home, a one-acre hilly   207
park closed in by a high chain-link fence, with trees, a pond, and a dark cave. He   224
spends his day walking, lying in the sun, playing with his toys, sleeping, sharpening   238
his claws, and stalking the water buffalo in a nearby enclosure. In the late afternoon,   253
the keepers feed Snowball three whole chickens, ten pounds of meat, ground bone, and   267
vitamins. He then sleeps in his night house until morning, when he begins his day by   283
splashing in the pond.   287

It is a shame not all white tigers were as fortunate as Snowball.   300

Turn the page.

Answer the questions below.

1 Which of the following is a statement of opinion?

  A Snowball was born in a wildlife park somewhere in the United States.

  (B) These are rare, beautiful creatures.

  C Tigers are solitary animals.

  D In the late afternoon, the keepers feed Snowball.

2 What would be the best way to find out how many captive white tigers exist in the world?

  F Ask someone at school.

  (G) Check on the Internet.

  H Go to the zoo and ask someone.

  J Read a book about India.

3 What conclusion can you draw from the information given in this selection?

  A All zoos in the United States have white tigers.

  (B) Humans have both harmed and helped white tigers.

  C White tigers eat more food than other tigers do.

  D White tigers sleep during the day and hunt at night.

4 Based on the selection, write a statement about Snowball that includes two opinions.

Answers may vary. Possible response: Snowball is a beautiful animal who seems happy in his home.

5 Write two statements of fact about why so few white tigers still exist.

Population growth has destroyed their natural home, and hunters have killed them.

Common Core State Standards

Questions 1–5: Literature 1. Refer to details and examples in a text when explaining what the text says explicitly and when drawing inferences from the text.

Name _____

Read the selection. Then answer the questions that follow.

Memories of Sugar Camp

Told by an Ojibwe Indian woman named Gawg in Minnesota in 1915.

In spring, we moved to sugar camp in the woods near Lake Superior.	13
First, Mama and I built our birch bark hut. Then we'd begin tapping the maple	29
trees. We pounded wooden taps into holes in the trunks. Then we attached pails to the	44
taps to catch the dripping sap. We tapped 300 trees, working like horses.	57
When the pails were full, we ran them to Grandma, who boiled the sap in big	73
kettles over a fire. It boiled down into a sweet, thick syrup. We poured this in the snow	91
to harden and then wrapped the sugar in birch bark.	101
We flavored our meat stews with this maple sugar, and I enjoyed lumps of it as	117
a treat. Sugaring was my favorite season, though we worked so hard.	129

Turn the page.

Answer the questions below.

1 What did they do *right after* they placed the taps in the tree trunks?

   A boiled down the sap

   (B) hung the pails on them

   C put kettles on the fire

   D ran the pails to Grandma

2 Which of these events happened *last?*

   F The sap ran down from the trees into pails.

   (G) The hardened sugar was wrapped in bark.

   H The maple sap was boiled down into syrup.

   J The thick syrup was poured on the snow.

3 The speaker compared herself and her family to horses to show that they

   A could run fast.

   B loved sugar lumps.

   (C) worked very hard.

   D lived mostly outside.

4 What happened later in the year after the speaker's family had made and wrapped up their maple sugar?

**Possible response: They used the sugar all year long when**

**they were cooking and as a sweet treat, too. Then they had**

**another sugar season the next year.**

Common Core State Standards

Questions 1–4: Informational Text 1. Refer to details and examples in a text when explaining what the text says explicitly and when drawing inferences from the text.

Name _____

Read the selection. Then answer the questions that follow.

First Lady

Michelle Robinson Obama strolls into a packed auditorium with a big smile on her face. The audience greets her warmly with a resounding round of applause. She steps up to the festooned podium and starts speaking. She is intelligent, caring, and strong. She is the First Lady of the United States, wife of President Barack Obama. She is a leader too.

Michelle Robinson was born on January 17, 1964, in Chicago. The family lived in a small, one-bedroom apartment. Her father worked as a city pump operator, and her mother became a secretary once the children were in high school. Michelle had one brother, Craig. The Robinsons taught their children that hard work and education are the keys to success.

Both Michelle and Craig went to college at Princeton. Michelle graduated in 1985 with honors. She earned a degree from Harvard Law School in 1988. Craig worked as a banker for a while, but then followed his dream to become a college basketball coach.

At first, Michelle Obama worked as a lawyer in a big Chicago law firm. There, she met Barack Obama. They married in 1992 and had daughters Malia and Sasha in 1999 and 2001.

Michelle Obama wanted to do more to assist people, and she left the big law firm in 1992. She held several important jobs at the University of Chicago, one of the big colleges in town. She led student services and the hospital's neighborhood programs.

When Barack Obama became the President in 2009, the family moved into the White House. Michelle Obama's success as a career woman and mother has inspired many people.

14
28
42
59
61
75
89
103
116
120
133
149
164
180
195
197
213
229
241
254
267
269

Turn the page.

Answer the questions below.

1 What did Michelle Obama do *right after* graduating from Princeton?

   A She worked at a law firm.

   (B) She went to a law school.

   C She became a secretary.

   D She managed a hospital.

2 According to the selection, what was Michelle Obama's first job?

   (F) lawyer

   G teacher

   H banker

   J doctor

3 What did Michelle Obama do *next* after leaving her first job?

   A moved her family into the White House

   B became a college basketball coach

   (C) worked at the University of Chicago

   D taught classes at Harvard Law School

4 What two things did Michelle Obama do in the same year?

   (F) She left the big law firm, and she got married.

   G She graduated from college and from law school.

   H She had two daughters, and she became President.

   J She went to law school and worked in a hospital.

5 Write two ways that Michelle Obama and her brother Craig were alike. Support your answer with details from the selection.

Possible response: They both went to college at Princeton, and later they both had jobs at colleges.

Common Core State Standards

Questions 1–5: Informational Text 1. Refer to details and examples in a text when explaining what the text says explicitly and when drawing inferences from the text.

Name _____

Read the selection. Then answer the questions that follow.

Watch Out

My brother, Joe, and I are fortunate to live next to a vast forest reserve with tall   17

trees, a stream, giant boulders, hills to climb, and a huge pond where we can fish. We   34

are allowed to go exploring as long as we promise to be cautious, stay together, and not   51

stray too far from the path. However, we get tired of Mom telling us to pay attention   68

and watch where we go. Joe is a fifth grader, I'm in the fourth grade, and we believe   86

we can take care of ourselves.   92

Yesterday we asked if we could go catch butterflies in the woods. Mom said, "Fine,   107

but be back for lunch. And Sarah, please watch out and don't be reckless. Try not to get   125

so bruised and scratched." Joe grinned because he seldom gets hurt.   136

We love to be in the woods, where the long branches of the trees form a green   153

ceiling. After climbing a steep hill, we came to a large meadow filled with colorful   168

wildflowers. Immediately Joe caught two butterflies. I was having no luck at all until I   183

looked down a little valley, where I saw hundreds of them.   194

Off I flew and suddenly slipped, falling and rolling down the hill. Joe came running   209

toward me yelling, "I'll help you."   215

"Watch out, Joe, it's really slippery." He tripped on a big rock, flew into the air, and   232

crashed into a giant log. He slowly picked himself up. I was scared. Joe had a big bump   250

on his head.   253

"You hurt yourself and Mom will be mad," I whimpered.   263

"Yes, but it's your fault. You were reckless as usual, and I was only trying to   279

rescue you."   281

I put my arm around him and we trudged home.   291

"I'm sorry, Joe. From now on I will listen to Mom."   302

Turn the page.

Answer the questions below.

1 What happened *right after* Joe and Sarah reached the large meadow?

   A They climbed a steep rise.

   (B) Joe caught two butterflies.

   C Sarah slipped down a hill.

   D They tripped on big rocks.

2 What happened just *before* Sarah apologized to Joe?

   F Mom told Sarah to watch out.

   (G) Joe told Sarah she was reckless.

   H Sarah caught butterflies for Mom.

   J Sarah told Joe to watch out.

3 Which of these events happened *first* in the story?

   A Sarah and Joe walked home.

   B Mom made a lunch for Joe.

   C Joe had tried to rescue Sarah.

   (D) Mom gave Sarah a warning.

4 Write a summary of the story using at least three clue words that show the order of the events.

Possible response: First, Sarah and Joe go butterfly hunting in the woods. Then Sarah falls down chasing butterflies. Next, Joe falls down and bumps his head while trying to rescue Sarah. Finally, they both head home, and Sarah apologizes to Joe for being reckless.

5 Tell two ways that Joe and Sarah are *alike* in the story. Tell two ways that they are *different*.

Possible response: Alike: Joe and Sarah both like butterfly hunting, and they both fall down and get hurt. Different: Sarah falls trying to catch butterflies, while Joe falls trying to save Sarah. Joe is in fifth grade, and Sarah is in fourth grade.

Common Core State Standards

Questions 1–3: **Literature 1.** Refer to details and examples in a text when explaining what the text says explicitly and when drawing inferences from the text. **Question 4: Literature 2.** Determine a theme of a story, drama, or poem from details in the text; summarize the text. **Question 5: Literature 3.** Describe in depth a character, setting, or event in a story or drama, drawing on specific details in a text (e.g., a character's thoughts, words, or actions).

Name _____

Read the selection. Then answer the questions that follow.

Teamwork

Last month our teacher assigned a history project. "You have two weeks to write a	15
three-page report on the Civil War, and you may choose to work alone or in teams."	31
I smiled at my best friend, Jan, who is really smart, and said, "Let's work together."	47
"No, Lisa, I want to do this by myself."	56
That surprised me because we always do everything together. My grades are not	69
great, but I am a good artist, and pictures can improve a report and make it more	86
interesting.	87
So I asked Andy and Mark, who are also very bright, to work with me.	102
The three of us enjoyed studying together. I noticed Jan looking at us in a funny	118
way when she saw us smiling and whispering over books at the library.	131
Our team earned an A, but Jan got a B. When I had lunch with her the next day she	151
said, "Next time let's all be a team, because four heads are even better than one."	167

Turn the page.

Answer the questions below.

1 Which generalization can you make from the facts in the selection?

   A It is fun to work with others.

   B It is smart to work alone.

   (C) Many minds are better than one.

   D To get something done well, do it yourself.

2 Which of the following is a valid generalization?

   F Pictures always improve a report.

   G Jan always wants to work alone.

   H Team members always have a good time.

   (J) Team members need to work together.

3 What happened *right after* Jan told Lisa that she wanted to work alone?

   (A) Lisa asked Andy and Mark to work with her.

   B Jan gave Lisa a funny look in the library.

   C Jan said she wanted to be on the team next time.

   D Lisa made pictures for the history project.

4 What is one generalization that appears in the story. What clue word makes it a generalization?

That surprised me because we always do everything together.

The clue word is "always."

Common Core State Standards

Questions 1–4: Literature 1. Refer to details and examples in a text when explaining what the text says explicitly and when drawing inferences from the text.

Name _____

Read the selection. Then answer the questions that follow.

Endless Energy

More and more people are thinking about how to get energy from sources other | 14
than oil, coal, or gas. Those fuels are generally dirty, and one day they will run out. | 31
Renewable energy means energy that will always be there (renewable = that can be made | 46
new again). The wind keeps blowing, the sun keeps shining, and the Earth keeps heating | 61
underground rocks. So as long as the Earth is here, those forms of energy will be here. | 78

People have been using wind power for a long time. Before engines were invented, | 92
ships had sails that filled with wind, moving them across the water. In some parts of the | 109
world, small sailing boats are still used for fishing. | 118

In the past, people generally built windmills to grind grain and to pump water. | 132
These windmills had sails that turned as they caught the wind. The sails turned a shaft | 148
that ran a pump or grinder. Today, large modern windmills have blades and work | 162
together in wind farms to produce electricity. | 169

Sunlight can also be used to make electricity. The sun shines on cells, which are | 184
often placed on the roof of a house or building. When the sun hits these cells, there is a | 203
reaction that makes electricity. As costs for electricity rise, more people are beginning | 216
to use energy from the sun. | 222

Geothermal energy is a way of using underground water that has been heated by | 236
rocks, which have themselves been heated by the great temperature of the Earth's core. | 250
This hot water is turned into steam, which then runs a machine that makes electricity. | 265

Using renewable energy is a good way to meet the electricity needs of the growing | 280
number of people in the world. | 286

Turn the page.

Answer the questions below.

1 Which generalization about renewable energy is made by the author?

(A) These forms of energy will always be there.

B In many parts of the world, wind is used to run motors.

C Few people know about renewable energy.

D Solar energy is generally cleaner than wind energy.

2 Which of the following is not a valid generalization?

F Sunlight can be used to create electricity.

G Wind power can be used to grind grain.

(H) Sources of coal will never run out.

J Underground hot water creates steam.

3 A hundred years ago wind power was generally used to

A run automobiles.

(B) pump water.

C warm houses.

D pump oil.

4 Which of these events happens *first* in the production of geothermal energy?

F Underground water is turned into electric steam.

G The rocks underground heat up underground water.

(H) The Earth's hot core heats up underground rocks.

J Steam is used to run machines that make electricity.

5 Make two generalizations about why finding sources of energy is becoming a problem in the world.

Answers may vary. Possible responses: The world's population is growing, and we are using electricity for more and more purposes. Also, costs for electricity are rising, and some sources of energy may run out.

Common Core State Standards

Questions 1–5: Informational Text 1. Refer to details and examples in a text when explaining what the text says explicitly and when drawing inferences from the text.

Name _____

Read the selection. Then answer the questions that follow.

The Gorilla

We know this great creature from zoos, books, and movies. It is the largest member	15
of a group of animals that includes monkeys, chimpanzees, and orangutans. An adult	28
male gorilla can weigh from three hundred to four hundred pounds. The gorilla's body	42
is covered with thick, dark hair except for its face, upper chest, fingers, palms, and the	58
soles of its feet. Its powerful jaws have big teeth for tearing and grinding food. Its arms	75
are long and very strong. An adult male gorilla could win a tug of war with six men.	93
Gorillas look a lot like people, with two arms and two legs and similar hands and	109
feet, but they walk on both their arms and legs, using the backs of their fingers like a	127
foot. The head and body look almost human.	135
Gorillas are found in only four forests of Africa, three in the lowlands and the	150
fourth in the mountains. Each day, a male gorilla will eat forty-five pounds of leaves,	165
twigs, bark, and grass. It gets moisture from the juicy plants and so drinks little water.	181
Once in a while it will munch on a bird's egg or an insect. Except for a nap at noon, it	202
eats from morning until night.	207
The main social group for gorillas is the family. The oldest male is the leader and is	224
responsible for the females with babies and the young males and females. Family life	238
is generally peaceful, kind, and considerate, with little fighting. The leader protects the	251
family and guides the group in the forest, which it shares with other families.	265
Today the gorilla is in danger. Forests are getting smaller because of the cutting of	280
trees, clearing of forests for homes, and grazing of cattle. In addition, hunters kill the	295
gorilla for food. Without the protection of these forests in Africa, this peaceful animal	309
will disappear.	311

Turn the page.

Answer the questions below.

1 **Which of the following generalizations is valid?**

(A) Gorillas are in danger because forests are being destroyed.

B The number of gorillas in the wild is increasing every year.

C Human hunters are the only threat to the survival of the gorilla.

D The greatest danger to gorilla families is other gorilla families.

2 **What generalization can you make about the gorilla's diet?**

F Gorillas eat only plants.

G The gorilla's main food is insects and bird's eggs.

(H) Gorillas get most of their moisture from plants.

J Gorillas eat most of their food at night.

3 **How does a gorilla spend most of its day?**

A sleeping in caves

B playing with other gorillas

C napping and playing

(D) looking for food

4 **Describe a typical day for a male gorilla, using at least three clue words that show the order of events. Use details from the selection in your answer.**

Possible response: First, the gorilla leads his large family to a good place to eat in the forest. Next he starts eating leaves, twigs, and bark. At about noon, he takes a nap. Later, he wakes up and starts eating again. He protects his family whenever he must do so.

5 **What generalization can you make about a gorilla's family life?**

Family life is generally peaceful, kind, and considerate.

Common Core State Standards

Questions 1–5: Informational Text 1. Refer to details and examples in a text when explaining what the text says explicitly and when drawing inferences from the text.

Name _____

Read the selection. Then answer the questions that follow.

Chelsea's Choice

Chelsea is a busy fourth grader who does very well in school and participates in | 15
many after-school activities. She's the captain of the soccer team and a volunteer at the | 30
city library, she babysits, and she takes piano lessons. | 39

Recently she tried out for the school play and was given the leading role, which | 54
was great news, but it meant she now had to rearrange her schedule. Rehearsals were | 69
planned for Tuesday and Thursday between 3:00 P.M. and 5:00 P.M. | 80

It was a problem. Soccer was her favorite sport, and Chelsea's teammates relied on | 94
her. She felt it was important to assist at the library. She cared about the Lopez children | 111
she babysat for and liked earning money. Also, she enjoyed studying the piano and | 125
could now play "New York, New York." So her big challenge was to determine how she | 141
could do it all. | 145

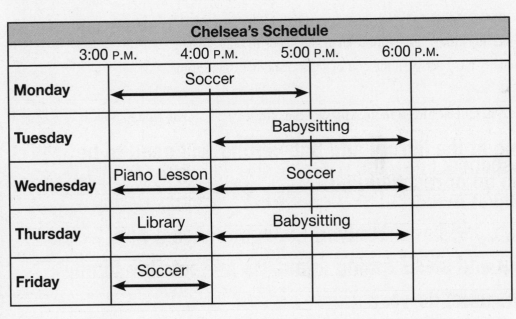

Chelsea's Schedule			
3:00 P.M.	**4:00** P.M.	**5:00** P.M.	**6:00** P.M.
Monday	← Soccer →		
Tuesday		← Babysitting →	
Wednesday	← Piano Lesson →	← Soccer →	
Thursday	← Library →	← Babysitting →	
Friday	← Soccer →		

Turn the page.

Answer the questions below.

1 Which activities will Chelsea not have to change?

(A) piano lesson and soccer

B soccer and babysitting

C babysitting and library

D library and piano lesson

2 On which day does Chelsea have the most free time?

F Monday

G Tuesday

H Thursday

(J) Friday

3 What is the *best* generalization you can make about Chelsea's schedule?

A Chelsea can easily fit into her afternoons all the things she likes to do.

B Chelsea has plenty of time to do her homework before dinner each day.

C Chelsea needs babysitting money more than she needs to play soccer.

(D) Chelsea is usually busy between the end of school and her dinner time.

4 Which activities will Chelsea need to give up or reschedule?

Volunteering at the library and babysitting will need to be either given up or rescheduled.

Common Core State Standards

Questions 1–4: Informational Text 7. Interpret information presented visually, orally, or quantitatively (e.g., in charts, graphs, diagrams, time lines, animations, or interactive elements on Web pages) and explain how the information contributes to an understanding of the text in which it appears.

Name _____

Read the selection. Then answer the questions that follow.

Wagon Train

The Oregon Trail was the route—or routes—used by thousands of settlers from | 14
the 1840s through the mid-1860s to reach the territory along the West Coast of North | 29
America. They made this challenging and dangerous two-thousand-mile trip in | 39
wagon trains, some made up of as many as twenty covered wagons. Most left from | 54
Independence, Missouri, in the spring when the winter snow had melted. Many kept a | 68
record of their five- to six-month odyssey. The following may have come from the diary | 83
of a young member of a pioneer family in 1865. | 93

May 1. We left Independence a month ago and are making good time, traveling | 107
more than 15 miles per day. Today we crossed the Platte River after the men spent | 123
several days building rafts to float the people and wagons across. | 134

June 20. We arrived in Fort Laramie after many weeks of slow and arduous | 148
travel through the Great Plains. Because of blinding dust storms followed by terrible | 161
thunderstorms, we only went a few miles a day. We need to rest here for a few days | 179
before attempting to cross the Rocky Mountains. | 186

August 25. We finally reached Fort Hall and everyone is exhausted. Crossing the | 199
mountains was a struggle. We borrowed one another's oxen to pull the wagons up the | 214
steep trail, but going down was trickier. To keep the wagons from slipping away, the | 229
men held on to them from behind with long ropes. | 239

October 1. Since leaving Fort Hall, we have followed the beautiful Columbia River | 252
all the way to Oregon City. It's been six months of unbelievable adventure. | 265

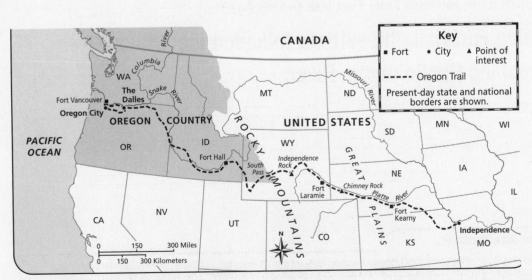

Turn the page.

Fresh Reads Unit 6 Week 5 OL

Answer the questions below.

1 Where did the wagon train run into dust storms?

   A near the Mississippi River

   (B) on the plains along the Platte River

   C near the Rocky Mountains

   D along the Columbia River

2 Using the scale, what is the distance from Fort Kearny to Fort Laramie?

   F 150 miles

   G 150 kilometers

   (H) 300 miles

   J 600 miles

3 Where were the settlers during most of their journey?

   A in mountains

   B on the Great Plains

   (C) close to rivers

   D near forts

4 Which of the following is a generalization from the selection?

   (F) Many kept a record of their five- to six-month odyssey.

   G Today we crossed the Platte River after days spent building rafts.

   H The men held on to the wagons from behind with ropes.

   J We need to rest here for a few days before crossing the mountains.

5 Using the map, describe the route from Fort Hall to Oregon City.

After leaving Fort Hall, the settlers followed the Snake River before reaching the Columbia River.

Common Core State Standards

Questions 1–5: Informational Text 7. Interpret information presented visually, orally, or quantitatively (e.g., in charts, graphs, diagrams, time lines, animations, or interactive elements on Web pages) and explain how the information contributes to an understanding of the text in which it appears.

Name _____

Read the selection. Then answer the questions that follow.

The Potato

The potato is a vegetable. It is also a *tuber,* which is the fat underground stem of	17
certain plants. It is easy to grow and filled with the fiber, minerals, and protein people	33
need in order to stay healthy. It also contains many vitamins needed for sustenance.	47
The potato was first grown in the cold, tall Andes Mountains of South America at	62
least five thousand years ago, but it was not until the time of Columbus, when explorers	78
brought the potato to Europe, that the rest of the world learned about this food.	93
At first, the potato was eaten only by farm animals and very poor people because of	109
prejudice against it. The potato is a member of the nightshade family of plants (as is the	126
tomato), and the leaves, in fact, are poisonous.	134
Then, in the 1700s, a Frenchman ate potatoes for the first time while a prisoner of	150
war in Germany. Thanks to him, the potato gained widespread popularity.	161
When the potato was brought to Ireland, it became the primary food of the poor	176
farmers of that country. Then, in the 1840s, a potato disease destroyed crops throughout	190
Europe. Over a four-year period, nearly a million people starved to death in Ireland,	204
and between 1847 and 1854 more than a million and a half people left Ireland and	220
came to America.	223
Potatoes can be cooked in many different ways—baked, boiled, fried, in a stew, or	238
mashed. No matter how they are prepared, they taste good and are healthful.	251

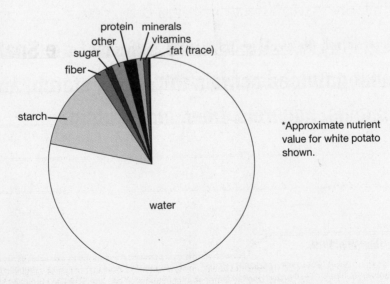

protein minerals
other vitamins
sugar fat (trace)
fiber
starch
water

*Approximate nutrient value for white potato shown.

Turn the page.

Answer the questions below.

1 The potato is mostly made up of
   A   fat and sugar.
   (B) water.
   C   starch.
   D   vitamins and minerals.

2 What would be the best title for the circle graph of the potato?
   F   The Potato
   (G) Food Value of the Potato
   H   What to Look for in the Potato
   J   History of the Potato

3 What generalization can you make about the potato based on this selection?
   A   Americans eat more potatoes than any other people.
   B   Potatoes can be ground into a fine flour for baking.
   (C) The potato has been an important food in history.
   D   Potatoes have fewer vitamins than other vegetables.

4 What additional graphic do you think would be helpful to include with this selection?

Answers may vary. Possible responses: A time line would be helpful to show the events that led to making the potato popular. Also, a picture of a potato plant might be helpful.

5 What did you learn from the circle graph that the passage did not tell you?

I learned that potatoes contain fat, sugar, starch, and water as well as vitamins, minerals, fiber, and protein.

Common Core State Standards

Questions 1–5: Informational Text 7. Interpret information presented visually, orally, or quantitatively (e.g., in charts, graphs, diagrams, time lines, animations, or interactive elements on Web pages) and explain how the information contributes to an understanding of the text in which it appears.

Fresh Reads   Unit 6 Week 5 A